WRITING

ANALYTICAL

ASSESSMENTS

IN SOCIAL WORK

CRITICAL
SKILLS FOR
SOCIAL WORK

Other books you may be interested in

Active Social Work with Children with Disabilities
By Julie Adams and Diana Leshone   ISBN 978-1-910391-94-5

Anti-racism in Social Work Practice
Edited by Angie Bartoli   ISBN 978-1-909330-13-9

Evidencing CPD – A Guide to Building Your Social Work Portfolio
By Daisy Bogg and Maggie Challis   ISBN 978-1-911106-14-2

Mental Health and the Criminal Justice System
By Ian Cummins   ISBN 978-1-910391-90-7

Modern Mental Health: Critical Perspectives on Psychiatric Practice
Edited by Steven Walker   ISBN 978-1-909330-53-5

Observing Children and Families: Beyond the Surface
By Gill Butler   ISBN 978-1-910391-62-4

Personal Safety for Social Workers and Health Professionals
By Brian Atkins   ISBN 978-1-909330-33-7

Positive Social Work: The Essential Toolkit for NQSWs
By Julie Adams and Angie Sheard   ISBN 978-1-909330-05-4

Practice Education in Social Work: Achieving Professional Standards
By Pam Field, Cathie Jasper & Lesley Littler   ISBN 978-1-911106-10-4

Psychosocial and Relationship-based Practice
By Claudia Megele   ISBN 978-1-909682-97-9

Social Media and Social Work Education
Edited by Joanne Westwood   ISBN 978-1-909682-57-3

Starting Social Work: Reflections of a Newly Qualified Social Worker
By Rebecca Joy Novell   ISBN 978-1-909682-09-2

The Critical Years: Child Development from Conception to Five
By Tim Gully   ISBN 978-1-909330-73-3

Understanding Substance Use: Policy and Practice
By Elaine Arnull   ISBN 978-1-909330-93-1

What's Your Problem? Making sense of Social Policy and the Policy Process
By Stuart Connor   ISBN 978-1-909330-49-8

Titles are also available in a range of electronic formats. To order please go to our website www.criticalpublishing.com or contact our distributor NBN International, 10 Thornbury Road, Plymouth PL6 7PP, telephone 01752 202301 or email orders@nbninternational.com

WRITING
ANALYTICAL
ASSESSMENTS
IN SOCIAL WORK

Chris Dyke

**CRITICAL
SKILLS FOR
SOCIAL WORK**

First published in 2016 by Critical Publishing Ltd
Reprinted in 2016 (four times)

British Library Cataloguing in Publication Data
A CIP record for this book is available from the British Library

ISBN: 978-1-911106-06-7

This book is also available in the following e-book formats:
MOBI: 978-1-911106-07-4
EPUB: 978-1-911106-08-1
Adobe e-book reader: 978-1-911106-09-8

Cover and text design by Out of House
Project Management by Out of House Publishing
Printed and bound in the UK by 4edge Limited

Critical Publishing
152 Chester Road
Northwich
CW8 4AL
www.criticalpublishing.com

MIX
Paper from
responsible sources
FSC   www.fsc.org   FSC® C013604

Contents

Help us to help you!

Our aim is to help you to become the best professional you can be. In order to improve your critical thinking skills we are pleased to offer you a **free booklet** on the subject.

Just go to our website www.criticalpublishing.com and click the link on the home page.

We have more free resources on our website which you may also find useful.

If you'd like to write a review of this book on Amazon, Books Etc., or Wordery, **we would be happy to send you the digital version of the book for free.**

Email a link to your review to us at admin@criticalpublishing.com, and we'll reply with a PDF of the book, which you can read on your phone, tablet or Kindle.

You can also connect with us on:

Twitter   @CriticalPub #criticalpublishing
Facebook   www.facebook.com/Critical-Publishing-456875584333404
Our blog   https://thecriticalblog.wordpress.com

Meet the author

Chris Dyke has worked in social care roles since 2002 and qualified as a social worker in 2006. He works as a visiting lecturer to universities and trainer to local and national organisations, while continuing to practice what he teaches, as an expert witness and assessor in the Family Courts.

He is naturally contrary and instinctively challenges accepted views (including his own) to ensure that he continues to develop.

Introduction

WHO THIS BOOK IS FOR

This book is for social workers who want to learn about people, who want to communicate what they've learned to someone else and who want to use what they've learned to inform their work.

These skills make writing a report much easier, and this book is for people who need to write reports. The written document is an important part, but *only* a part, of understanding a person.

Student social workers and newly qualified ('ASYE') social workers might find this book particularly useful. I've written thinking of my students at Goldsmiths and Royal Holloway, now and in the future, but also of myself as a student. I've tried to write to the younger me, with a guide to what I wish I'd known at that stage – most of which I've since learned the hard way.

For more experienced social workers, some of the advice might seem obvious – indeed, it might seem obvious to students. But everything I've written is something I wish more social workers knew. While students and newly qualified social workers may find the content more enlightening, it's the workers who've been practising for many years who can better understand (and recognise) the scenarios. This may help them reflect on their own practice during their continuing journey of development. I've learned a lot writing this book, so I'm hoping there's something in it for everyone.

Managers and educators, too, might find useful ideas, although I'd warn against treating any of my advice as dogmatic or definitive. The strength of social work is in its diversity of personalities and methods, and while my techniques might be useful for many people, I've only been able to develop them because I've been allowed the freedom to try out new ideas. I never stop trying to learn more, so I intend to adapt and improve the advice in this book – I'd encourage other people to do the same.

My own experiences come from a decade in children's social work, so I was tempted to write the book specifically for this half of the profession (I considered the title *Writing Analytical Assessments in Children's Social Work* at first), to make sure I didn't leave adults' specialists feeling short-changed.

However, writing solely for children's social workers would pander to an increasing and worrying trend towards segregating the profession (Unwin and Hogg 2012). The importance of a generic skill base, rather than an exclusive children's or adults' focus, runs through social work's history (Hatton et al. 2007), hence the fierce resistance of the profession to government proposals to split the degree course (Narey 2014). The skills discussed in this book are applicable to either field, with the exception of the **Appendix**. While many of my case studies are based on experience of children's social work, I have used these to make generic points.

WHAT THIS BOOK IS FOR

This isn't the book I planned to write. I thought it would be a skills-based, pragmatic guide, steering clear of the wider political and ethical debates in social work (discussed more in Chapters 4–6). But I soon found it's impossible to write about one without the other: every skill you learn, every decision you make and every word you use in social work comes with value judgements. To understand a person you need to know about their context, and about *your* context and why you are working the way you are. This wider awareness is not a distraction from practical skills, but a foundation for them.

On reflection, maybe I was initially reluctant to discuss the political context because of self-consciousness: as a white, male, middle-class, cisgender professional, did I have the right to talk about oppression and discrimination? I soon realised this was the wrong mindset: as a privileged, empowered citizen (with the added privilege of having my words in print), I not only had a right, but a *duty* to highlight the power structures and themes affecting social work.

I had a further dilemma when writing about the political and ethical context of social work, and about the underpinning theories, which was how to do so competently. To ignore these concepts would be ignorant; to mention them briefly risked incorrectly summarising them or treating them as footnotes; to address them with the depth they deserve would create a whole other book. I have tried to strike a balance, but for anyone encountering the wider themes in social work for the first time, this book should be the start rather than the end of your learning: see the **Taking it further** sections in each chapter for recommended further reading.

I then worried that, by focusing on assessments, this book could come across as managerial or technocratic. Social workers need to understand who they're working with, so 'assessment' is an important skill. But it's only a small part of social work, a profession created to improve people's lives and to improve society. Obsessing over assessments can turn social work into a monitoring and surveillance activity, not a transformative one.

I've tried to tie the nuts-and-bolts, practical guidance in this book to its eventual aim. There's a 'thread' connecting the humdrum and the values of the work: for example, keeping your emails and documents organised allows you to spend less time on administration, and respond to people quicker, allowing you to spend a greater quantity and quality of time with service users. Clear writing and precise analysis create, and communicate, a better understanding of the people you work with, so you can work with them better. There is no contradiction between being an efficient social worker and a principled one, quite the opposite: a worker with solid values can only put them into practice if they are organised; and a practical social worker will only do good work if it has a coherent value base.

There are many more themes that this book only touches on. I have focused on what to do before contact with service users, and what to do with your information afterwards. The gap in the middle is how to have those conversations and how to build relationships. While the skills I cover can help, I've deliberately avoided a lengthy exploration of interviewing skills and relationship-based social work, because others cover the subject so much better. In the **Taking it further** section, I've pointed out some more in-depth guides, including references to general skill guides (Ruch et al. 2010; Ross 2011; Riggall 2012) as well as interview tools and guidance for particular circumstances (Reder et al. 2003; Goodman 2007; Richards 2009; Ferguson 2011; Aspinwall-Roberts 2012; Tait 2012; Nicholas 2015).

SOCIAL WORK ASSESSMENTS

I based my practical advice on research findings about what makes the difference to the quality of an assessment.

Turney et al. (2011) found that poor-quality assessments, which lead to poorer outcomes for service users (Farmer and Owen 1995), typically feature:

- gaps and inaccuracies in the information;

- description rather than analysis of the information presented;

- little or no understanding of the service user's perspective.

Conversely, good-quality assessments:

- contain full, concise, relevant and accurate information;

- include a chronology and/or family and social history;

- ensure that the service user remains central;

- make good use of information from a range of sources;

- include analysis that makes clear links between the recorded information and plans for intervention (or decisions not to take any further action).

THE CHAPTERS

Chapter 1 is a guide to the practicalities and concepts of writing a chronology, including specific advice on chronologies for court. It comes first for a reason: the chronology helps to frame and plan out your assessment.

Chapter 2 introduces genograms and ecomaps: how they're constructed, how to use them and what part they can play in your assessment.

Chapter 3 explores how to get the work done in the reality of a busy working environment with a demanding caseload. This chapter is based more on personal experience and 'what's worked for me', but without including this advice, the book would be incomplete.

Chapter 4 looks at writing style, techniques and common flaws, to help communicate your knowledge effectively. It includes an introduction to the significance of language in anti-oppressive practice.

Chapter 5 discusses the analytical portion of your work: how to avoid common pitfalls, how to make the argument sound and how to make it useful for service users and the people working with them. This chapter includes a discussion on plans.

Chapter 6 summarises the key points and themes of the book.

I have included only one chapter specifically aimed at children's social workers – an **Appendix** on writing for child care proceedings, focusing on the local authority social work evidence template. This is a national standard document so should be applicable nationwide. I can only apologise for not including an adults' guide to writing a key report (e.g., a Court of Protection COP2) but this would be outside my expertise. The Social Care Institute for Excellence (SCIE) do, however, provide useful guidance (SCIE 2011).

I have used the term 'service user' to talk about the people social workers work with: children, their carers or vulnerable adults. In a book about writing, it's a clunky phrase that doesn't 'flow' as it should. It also suggests a process-driven, consumerist idea of a person 'receiving a service'. However, it is an instantly recognisable term in the profession, and preferable to the alternative 'client', which carries even more assumptions about the nature of their relationship with the social worker. I have therefore used 'service user' for expediency and clarity.

Wherever I have drawn on my own casework for examples, I have anonymised and, in some cases, fictionalised details to avoid identifying the people involved.

I have used research evidence to support my ideas wherever possible. Where I have relied on my own personal experience, or on my own smaller-scale (unpublished) studies, I have said so.

REFLECTION AND ACKNOWLEDGEMENTS

This book, like my practice, may appeal to people with very different philosophies to mine. My 'efficient' work appeals to those who see social work through a performance-management lens. I believe in assessing people promptly, not because of performance targets, but because people shouldn't be left in limbo (or worse, in danger) any longer than it takes to help them. I believe in being organised and comprehensive in order to free up the time and space to do useful, informed work with people, not because efficiency is an aim in itself.

My assessments 'meet timescales' and 'comply with criteria'. But these are administrative side-effects of my work: the real aim is to create a balanced, useful understanding of someone's situation, to inform the social work practice that can improve their lives and to do so in a timely fashion.

There is some overlap between the two philosophies: a social worker who never sees a service user and does belated, poor-quality work does badly on the performance-management measure as well as any qualitative measure of their work. A social worker who does sensitive, analytical, useful work in a short timeframe performs well on both measures. But this doesn't mean the two measures are interchangeable.

Writing a book about writing carries an inherent risk: if it's poorly written, the point is lost and the advice is discredited.

It also leads to the uncomfortable question: do I always follow my own advice? I can only wish that were true: I've learned more from my mistakes than my successes, and learned through reflection, the guidance of others (too numerous to mention) and through trial and error.

I'm indebted to the following for reading my drafts and giving feedback: Karen Goodman, Kevin Farmer, Joanne Rabbitte, Shaheen Syedain, Nicola Hutchins, Georgia McKay (who also organised my references), Tony Dougan, Sharon Jennings and Joan Fletcher. I am also indebted to the many authors and researchers I have quoted – I hope I've done their ideas justice. In particular, I hope I've fairly represented the work of the authors I particularly admire: Eileen Munro, Marion Brandon, Sue White, Ray Jones and others have all influenced my practice and I can't recommend their work highly enough. Any errors are of course my own.

TAKING IT FURTHER

Aspinwall-Roberts, E (2012) *Assessments in Social Work with Adults*, Oxford University Press

Davies, M (ed.) (2012) *Social Work with Adults*, Palgrave Macmillan

Ferguson, H (2011) *Child Protection Practice*, Palgrave Macmillan

Goodman, R (1997) The strengths and difficulties questionnaire: a research note, *Journal of Child Psychology and Psychiatry*, 38, 581–586, also www.sdqinfo.com

Nicholas, J (2015) *Conducting the Home Visit in Child Protection*, Palgrave Macmillan

Reder, P, Duncan, S and Lucey, C (2003) *Studies in the Assessment of Parenting*, Routledge

Richards, L (2009) DASH risk assessment for domestic violence, www.dashriskchecklist.co.uk and www.safelives.org.uk

Riggall, S (2012) *Using Counselling Skills in Social Work*, Learning Matters

Ross, J (2011) *Specialist Communication Skills for Social Workers*, Palgrave Macmillan

Ruch, G, Ward, A and Turney, D (2010) *Relationship-Based Social Work: Getting to the Heart of Practice*, Jessica Kingsley

Tait, A (2012) *Direct Work with Vulnerable Children*, Jessica Kingsley

REFERENCES

Farmer, E and Owen, M (1995) *Child Protection Practice: Private Risks and Public Remedies: A Study of Decision-Making, Intervention and Outcome in Child Protection Work*, HMSO

Hatton, A, Brown, K and Parker, J (2007) Why we must keep out all-rounders, *Professional Social Work*, November, 10–11

Narey, M (2014) *Making the Education of Social Workers Consistently Effective: Report of Sir Martin Narey's Independent Review of the Education of Children's Social Workers*, Department for Education

SCIE (2011) SCIE Guide 42: Good Practice Guide on Accessing the Court of Protection www.scie.org.uk/publications/guides/guide42

Turney, D, Platt, D, Selwyn, J and Farmer, E (2011) *Social Work Assessment of Children in Need: What Do We Know? Messages From Research*, Department for Education

Unwin, P and Hogg, R (2012) *Effective Social Work with Children and Families: A Skills Handbook*, Sage

1 Chronologies: The start and heart of a good assessment

WHAT THIS CHAPTER COVERS

- How chronologies fit into assessments.

- Advantages to writing a chronology first.

- How chronologies help you build relationships.

- How chronologies help avoid 'start-again syndrome'.

- How to put a chronology together.

- Why it can't be automated.

- How chronologies help you analyse.

- Why (and how) to focus a chronology on the person.

- The differences between chronologies and case notes.

- Chronologies for the Family Court.

- Examples of chronologies for different stages of your work.

CHRONOLOGIES AND ASSESSMENTS

Assessments are an exercise in professional judgement. They can't be produced by a computer, or 'pulled through' from case notes and other documents. They require a social worker to use their knowledge, their skills and their professional discretion to fashion raw information into a useful piece of work.

Chronologies are also exercises in professional judgement. They don't require the same depth of analysis as the assessment, but they are an indispensable part of it. Just like an assessment, a chronology requires professional knowledge, skill and discretion. And just like an assessment, they can't be produced by a computer. They too require a social worker's skill.

So why, in many teams, are chronologies treated as an administrative task, a tiresome bureaucratic exercise to be done as an afterthought? Why are so many teams prepared to delegate chronologies to unqualified staff, who would never be expected to write an assessment? Why do so many workers say 'I've done the assessment, now I've got to do the chronology' when the one is impossible without the other?

Part of this is a misunderstanding about what a chronology is for and what case notes are for. In this chapter I hope to put this confusion to bed.

I've included this chapter first because a chronology is the first thing I ever write when I'm writing an assessment. While there's much more to an assessment than just the facts, without the facts you don't have much.

A chronology *tells the story*. It should tell the reader what's happened to a child, what's happened to an adult, what's happened to a family. It doesn't analyse in itself, but it gives you the raw materials for analysis. *If you haven't done a chronology, you haven't done an assessment.*

I have used 'fragments' of chronologies in this chapter, to make one specific point at a time. At the end of the chapter, I have included some examples of 'full' chronologies for fictional cases.

THE SAME FOR EVERYONE?

Different teams will use chronologies differently, and many adults' services teams don't use them at all. You may always find a use for a chronology, or you may find it unnecessary (when your role is entirely around meeting a physical disability need, for example). However, I would strongly recommend a chronology for any case involving an element of investigation or establishing a history.

WHY YOU SHOULD WRITE THE CHRONOLOGY AT THE START

Over the next few sections I'll argue for why writing the chronology first is essential. In Chapter 3, I'll show how this is not only realistic (even when faced with a high caseload) but an important part of managing your workload.

For clarity: 'doing the chronology first', doesn't mean the finished article. Usually this means a rough copy, sometimes a scribbled set of notes, always a 'working document' that you'll update before you complete a report.

You may work on duty desks where you have to head out in response to a new emergency. You'll have a matter of minutes between hearing the family name for the first time, and leaving the office. It would be understandable to claim 'I've got no time for a chronology, I've got an emergency to deal with/a child to protect/a vulnerable adult to accommodate'. But remember that when you get 'out there', you have a *decision* to a make. A decision that needs to be based on as much useful information as possible. While it may sound daunting to spend time working on a chronology when an emergency is unfolding, it's not as daunting as making a major decision based on incomplete information.

In that situation, it helps to spend some time reading the referral, scanning any previous records on the service users involved, noting down some key dates and pieces of information (and creating a genogram – see Chapter 2), and contacting other professionals (where possible) to ask any crucial questions about gaps in my knowledge. Your 'chronology' might be little more than a scrawled set of points on a notepad, but it will still be invaluable, and it gives you a start towards producing a 'formal' chronology later on.

Where you're not so pressed for time, you can spend longer on a typed chronology – time you would otherwise have spent later on anyway.

Whatever the situation, I'd always recommend starting a chronology before leaving the office.

HOW CHRONOLOGIES HELP YOUR RELATIONSHIP WITH SERVICE USERS

A lot of your work can go more smoothly because you've done a chronology. One of the most common complaints I've heard is: 'I hate having a new social worker, it's always the same – I've got to tell my whole story to another person, start again from scratch.'

When you work with a family, usually you won't be the first professional to do so. You might be the latest in a long line of professionals, and by no means the last. There will always be some information that is lost to you – sitting only in the head of the social worker who heard it. However, if you're a local authority social worker (or working for a similarly large organisation), you will often have a wealth of old files, reports and chronologies at your disposal.

This is about much more than efficiency or thoroughness. It's about showing the person in front of you the basic respect of bothering to read about them before you visit. You're not meeting them in your personal capacity, you're meeting as the representative of an organisation. If your organisation knows something, you should know it.

Social workers frequently complain of the lack of time to meet service users. This makes it even more vital to make the most of every minute with someone. The time should be spent either learning about someone or helping them (hopefully both). Sometimes this will be indirect, sometimes achieved in a roundabout way. But a visit should never be happening just to say you've done a visit. You certainly shouldn't be wasting someone's time, and showing them a lack of basic consideration, by asking them things that you could have learned from your own files.

This is also about something more fundamental – how social workers come across to their service users and to the public at large. Aldridge (2002) catalogues a range of slurs used against social workers in the press: 'naïve', 'bumbling' and 'incompetent' come up frequently.

The British tabloids have a distinctive style, and social workers are not the only professionals to incur their wrath. But the 'meme' of the social worker as an incompetent professional persists. Other professionals might be slandered as 'arrogant', or 'greedy' but an attack on the competence of the profession is much more damaging – it undermines the trust that wider society (and individual families) have in the social worker's ability to come to a wise decision. This continual demeaning of the profession reached the point where it was necessary for the president of the Family Division of the High Court to spell out that social workers should be treated as experts in their field (BASW 2014), in an effort to encourage public and professionals alike to regard a social worker's word as valuable.

Every social worker has a part to play in reversing this damaging portrayal. Every social worker has the responsibility to show genuine competence: to their service users, to their colleagues and to society at large. This starts with the first contact a social worker makes.

Consider these two scenarios:

Scenario 1

You are working in an adults' substance misuse team. Mr Smith comes to see a duty worker, feeling very depressed because he has just relapsed and been arrested for a public order offence while drunk.

Mr Smith is angrily asking to see someone, so you rush downstairs. You ask him his address and phone number. He replies angrily, saying he gave these details to your colleague earlier that day. You ask him if he's relapsed before. He says yes, he's been battling alcoholism for 20 years and since he first stopped drinking five years ago, he's relapsed three times. He says that you should know this since he's been in this office each time. He says he's fed up telling the same story to different people. He agrees to come back for an appointment but he shakes his head as he leaves. He doesn't turn up to see a counsellor the next week.

Scenario 2

You're a duty worker in a children's safeguarding team. Your manager asks you to go to a school to interview 12-year-old Eric who said his father hit him with a belt. Your manager tells you to get a move on as the police are already on their way.

However, you still make sure you check the system and quickly scan the last few assessments. This takes you 20 minutes. You note down the dates of three previous occasions Eric has said his father beats them, and one previous occasion where his older brother Darren said their father beats them. In each case, the investigation was ended after the children said they'd made it up and the teacher was exaggerating what they'd said.

When you get to the school, Eric says it didn't really happen, the teacher had made it up, and there was no problem at home. The police (who don't know about two of the previous allegations) are content to leave it at that. You ask Eric about the other times he's said this. Eric says that Darren told him that when he told the school, dad beat him even harder. He says Darren told him never to let a social worker know what happened, or he'd hit him too – he doesn't want the family broken up.

PREPARING IS NOT PRE-JUDGING

Everything in this chapter about gathering information before meeting a service user does **not** mean making up your mind before you go out.

While you should read the information first, remember that:

- It may be wrong or biased.

- It may be incomplete or lack context.

- It may be out of date.

- It may no longer be important.

Your understanding requires listening with an open mind to what people say. Knowing the history means that you pay attention to what they leave unsaid, as well as what they say.

Always be ready to have your ideas dismantled by new evidence. A chronology doesn't tell you everything that's happening in someone's life, it just helps you not to miss the obvious.

It's not a case of 'I don't have the time to read the files and start a chronology'; it's a case of 'I don't have time not to'. Having to do the same work later, after a problem has got worse, wastes a lot more time than the minutes spent developing a basic understanding of the family history.

Imagine an exchange like this:

> '... and then he punched me, and walked out shouting names at me from outside. So I started having a drink after that, and I guess I got very drunk and angry. I know I shouldn't but it just happened that way.'

> 'I'm sorry to hear about that. It sounds like what happened three years ago, with Andrew.'

> 'Yeah, yeah it does. I hadn't thought about it like that.'

Immediately, on a first visit, this service user knows you've at least done your homework. She knows that you care enough to save her the discomfort of telling you her life story all over again. She knows you're thinking about patterns in her life, maybe trying to find ways to break a cycle (the above exchange leads naturally into a conversation about this). She also knows that you know something about her.

Showing you've prepared for a visit doesn't prove to a service user that you know everything about them, but it does show that you know something.

This matters where a service user isn't telling the truth.

CHRONOLOGIES AS A TOOL TO AVOID 'START-AGAIN SYNDROME'

While there are many reasons someone would avoid telling the truth to a social worker, two (non-exhaustive) categories stand out:

1. Because they don't trust the social worker to make good use of their personal information.
2. Because they have caused someone else harm.

In the first case, showing an understanding of the family history is one of many ways a social worker can demonstrate their competence and integrity.

In the second case, while the interviewee may still try to mislead the social worker, the knowledge that the social worker will at least check their facts may play on their mind. Someone is less likely to tell the social worker 'I've always been a law-abiding citizen, I don't believe in violence' when they have a long history of violent offences and they know the social worker is in the habit of checking information.

Some readers might find it implausible that someone would try and deceive a social worker so brazenly. But it happens a lot.

When you write basic chronologies, based on reading the case file, you'll often be left with something like this:

Date	Information
Nov 2014	Mr Jones hit Mrs Jones in front of James and Rhona. No further action taken.
Feb 2015	Mr Jones hit Mrs Jones in front of James and Rhona. Social Services concluded no further action, but that a child protection conference would take place if it happened again.
Aug 2015	Mr Jones hit Mrs Jones during a drunken argument. Social Services warned him that they would hold a child protection conference if this happened again.
Dec 2015	Mr Jones strangled Mrs Jones in front of James and Rhona. Social Services completed an investigation and warned the couple that they would hold a child protection conference if this happened again.
(this referral)	Mr Jones hit Mrs Jones…

On your first visit, unless you're telling Mr and Mrs Jones about arranging a child protection conference, you lose a lot of credibility. In this (basic) example, it's highly unlikely that the previous social workers in August and December have read the files.

THE PREVIOUS SOCIAL WORKER'S RECOMMENDATIONS

If a previous social worker concludes their report with 'If X happens again, we will do Y', and then X happens again, does your response have to be Y?

Strictly speaking, no: you are a professional with your own professional judgement. You may disagree with the previous social worker's analysis, or the situation may have changed (e.g., the perpetrator of abuse may have fled the country or died by the time you write your report).

However, the view of the previous social worker represents the view of your organisation, as does yours. Therefore, at the very least you need to justify why you're taking a different view. For example: 'The previous report recommends we do Y if X happens. X has happened. However, I am not recommending Y because …'

Disagreeing with the previous recommendations may be justified. Ignoring them, however, is not.

Similarly, chronologies can guard against 'start-again syndrome'. Marion Brandon and colleagues (2008) coined this term for neglect cases where social workers are satisfied by positive changes without realising that this is the same small change that has happened before.

Date	Information
Jan to Jul 2013	Child protection plan due to the home being persistently dirty, with dog faeces on the walls. Family worked with Family Support Service. Home condition improved significantly. Case closed.
Aug 2014 to Jan 2015	Child in need plan due to the children being smelly, poorly fed and the home being dirty. Family Help Service helped the family achieve positive change and the concerns reduced significantly.
Sep 2015 to Jan 2016	New referral due to the dirty state of the home and the children being neglected. Referral made to Family Improvement Service. Family Improvement Service workers praised the family's commitment to change – the home improved substantially and the concerns were addressed. Case closed in January 2016.
May 2016 (this referral)	The school have referred to Social Services because the children are dirty and hungry when they come to school. The home–school liaison officer found the home very dirty. *Your manager has asked you to do an assessment and consider the family for the new Family Welfare Service.*

Writing this chronology, two things leap out:

1. A support service may have little long-term effect, judging from the three previous periods of neglect followed by short-term improvement followed by deterioration.
2. The periods of time between improvement and deterioration are *shortening* (13 months; eight months; four months…), suggesting that the family may be finding it even harder to cope.

We can experience a cognitive bias called an 'Availability Heuristic' where we place more emphasis on the information most available to us, and find information more accessible if it is 'vivid' and emotionally charged (Tversky and Kahneman 1973). In social work, this means we are more likely to form a view based on what we have recently seen and heard ourselves (e.g., on a home visit, talking to the family, or the most recent referral) than from information that is 'dry' and detached (e.g., written in professional jargon in an old file), even when the latter may better represent the service user's experience. This is linked to the 'Picture Superiority Effect' (Nelson et al. 1976), where we are more likely to hold a notion in our mind if we have experienced it as an image rather than as written words. A social worker may go on a visit to a beautiful, clean home, talk to polite, articulate parents and a child who says that 'everything's fine', and come back with a positive impression of the family. Even when they later consider the long list of violent incidents at the home, the 'vividness' of their own experience is stronger.

But isn't this just an argument for reading the old case files, *not* for doing a chronology? Not quite:

• A chronology 'nudges' you towards a comprehensive review of the history. When you start writing a chronology, and find an important gap, your curiosity leads you to ask questions about what happened during that gap. When you find a reference to another part of the country, you naturally want to check their records (and make the relevant requests). When you find a partial but important reference (e.g., a long time admitted to hospital; a period in care) you want to find out why this happened and what came of it. It doesn't give you all the answers, but it encourages you to start asking the questions.

• The lining-up of information so you can see what has happened before/after particular events. This doesn't prove causation but it suggests possibilities for you to explore.

STARTING A CHRONOLOGY

Even before you've started your assessment in earnest, you can include:

• **Dates of birth.** The most important things that ever happen in someone's life are their own birth, death and the start/end of major relationships, and the same events for those closest to them. Including the dates of birth has an interesting 'nudge' effect as well: it encourages you to consider the time between that date and now. For example, including parents' dates of birth starts you asking: what's happened since? If they were born in 1980, their child was born in 2008 and the first referral is 2010, then what happened between 1980 and 2010? As ever, a chronology doesn't give you the answers, but it encourages you to ask the questions.

• Whose dates of birth to include is a matter of judgement. You might start with both parents' dates of birth, by default. However, if you're also considering the roles of the grandparents, and their own lifestyles, then you'd probably include grandparents' dates of birth too. I once saw a chronology starting in 1900 with the birth of the great-great-great-grandparents. It made sense for that case: a family with an ingrained and complex pattern of sexual abuse down the generations. It's important to know where an adult has come from, what their experience has been, and whether current problems are new or 'one-off's or whether they represent something persistent going back decades.

ENTRIES MORE THAN TWO YEARS OLD

President of the Family Division Sir James Munby (2013) said that court chronologies should be 'succinct… three or four pages at the most' and that 'documents need not be served or listed if they are older than two years… with a concentration on what is relevant, what is central, what is key, rather than what is peripheral or merely historical'.

Local authorities have interpreted this correctly as advice to focus chronologies on the two years before issuing proceedings. But this doesn't rule out important information before that date. See later section on **Chronologies for the Family Court** for further details.

- **Police reports.** Police reports provide details about a recent referral, and often contain a list (in chronological order) of arrests and convictions (these are generally not suitable for use in court, but are useful as an assessment tool until you receive more formal checks). They have the advantage of being contemporaneous (they include the date the offence happened, rather than just when they received the report or secured a conviction) and frequently contain most of the more worrying moments from someone's life.

- **Referral information.** The referral itself might contain useful information: how long something's been going on, when something happened, etc. Always note when something *happened* rather than when something was *recorded*.

- **Old chronologies.** The writers of previous chronologies may not have had guidance on completing a chronology. Some of the documents entitled 'chronology' won't help you and won't be comprehensive. Some of them may be little more than enhanced case notes. However, they're a good place to start and will contain at least some useful background information to include in your own document. Be prepared to 'follow the stepping stones' back to a source if the information is unclear.

- **What people tell you.** You're writing the story of someone's life. That person (and their family) will be the best source of that information. For most of people's lives, they don't have a social worker or another professional hovering around – some of the most important pieces of information for a chronology (starts and ends of relationships, traumatic but secret events, etc.) will only come from conversations with the people involved.

- **Other people's information.** By default, it helps to include key information on people within the service user's household or who are otherwise central to their life. This is a matter of judgement, but consider these examples:

Chronology for an assessment of Jimmy, age 6	
Date	Information
Aug 2014	Jimmy's half-sister Eleanor accuses their father of sexually abusing her. Social Services cannot substantiate the allegation so no further action is taken, but Eleanor's mother cuts off contact with her father.
Aug 2016	Jimmy starts displaying very disturbed and violent behaviour in school including simulating sex with other children and slapping them.

Chronology for an assessment of Edward, aged 89	
Date	Information
Jan 2009	Edward's son and daughter-in-law have their son removed into foster care due to serious neglect. Their pet dogs are also removed by the RSPCA.
Sep 2016	Anonymous allegation from a neighbour that Edward is living with his son and daughter-in-law and being locked in a small room all day while they spend his pension.

In both cases, key information relevant to your assessment is recorded in someone else's file.

You may be told not to use this on confidentiality grounds, and that the information about the other person (Eleanor, or Edward's grandson) is private to them. This information may have to be removed when the information is shared in future, but at the time when you're making your enquiries you need to know it. Having to redact information at a later date is preferable to missing vital information that helps your investigations.

USING PROFESSIONAL JUDGEMENT TO DEVELOP A CHRONOLOGY: WHY A COMPUTER CAN'T (YET) DO IT FOR YOU

Some local authorities try to automate the process, by programming their data system to 'pull through' key events into chronologies. This sounds tempting. Organisations hold enormous databases with vast reams of information, so why not use the computing power of the database to make a chronology for you?

But current products can't make you a chronology. For a start, they can't make sense of prose. For example, you've been given a new case in September 2016, and you find an old assessment, dated November 2014. You read the assessment, and find the following section:

Background
Mr Muhammed has been diabetic for nine years, but his condition got a lot worse when he was 25, when he started drinking heavily after the end of his relationship. Two months ago he was admitted to hospital and briefly went into a coma.

This is the sort of thing you'd include in your rough chronology, something like this:

Date	Information
14.09.1987	Mr Muhammed born.
2007 approx.	Mr Muhammed diagnosed with diabetes.
2012/2013?	Mr Muhammed's relationship with X ended. He started drinking heavily and his diabetes got worse from this time.
Sep 2014	Mr Muhammed was admitted to hospital and briefly went into a coma.

(Note the provisional 'tone' of the entries – they act as a prompt to find out more, if relevant, about who his ex-partner was, and exactly when these events took place. The date of birth would have been clear on the files.)

No information system I've worked with could latch onto the information in that report and put it into a chronology in the way a social worker can (although one day they may be able to). Computers are good at pulling through basic details: dates of birth, dates of referrals, dates of meetings and when reports were completed. This doesn't paint the picture that's so crucial for a good chronology.

Note also the willingness to use *approximate* dates, even approximate *years*, where an event is very significant but lacks a precise date. Again, this is hard for a computer to 'pull through' from other data.

INCLUDE THE POSITIVE

Service users rightly complain that social workers tend to focus on the negative in their lives, and miss what's good. This applies to chronologies. Use what service users tell you about things that went well, and particularly happy moments or periods of time, to paint a more balanced picture. Include the negative and dangerous moments, but recognise where there are long gaps between incidents and that life may have been going well then.

CHRONOLOGIES AS A TOOL TO MAKE CONNECTIONS

Where a chronology stops being a bureaucratic exercise, and starts to provide the framework for your assessment, is when you start looking at correlations between events – yet another reason why a computer cannot produce a chronology, and why it would make no sense for an unqualified colleague to create the chronology for you: professional judgement is required to identify possible connections and to incorporate them into your report. (Note that a correlation does **not** prove a causation. X happening just before Y does not prove that X caused Y. It does, however, give you a question to consider in your assessment.)

Let's say you start your chronology with the following information from your files:

Date	Information
17.01.1982	Ms Martin born to parents Josephine Martin and Carl Graham.
18.04.1996	Referral from school to social care after Ms Martin (14) became very drunk and cut her wrists. No further action by social care – referred to CAMHS.
02.07.2012	Jeremy Martin born.
05.09.2013	Referral from police to social care after Ms Martin (who police thought was depressed) was stopped for drink-driving with Jeremy (14mths) in the car. No further action taken.
03.05.2015	Referral from police after Ms Martin called them to her home, asking them to remove Mr Jones, her partner, from her address. No further allegations made, no further action.
18.04.2016 (this referral)	Referral from police after a fight between Ms Martin and Mr Jones. Both of them had been drinking. Mr Jones smashed a mirror before leaving.

And then you add information from your visit (in bold/italic), based on what Ms Martin told you:

Date	Information
17.01.1982	Ms Martin born to parents Josephine Martin and Carl Graham.
1996 approx.	*Ms Martin says her parents started fighting a lot before they separated, when she was 'about 14'.*
18.04.1996	Referral from school to social care after Ms Martin (14) became very drunk and cut her wrists. No further action by social care – referred to CAMHS.
Oct 2011 approx.	(inferred from birth date) Ms Martin became pregnant.
Jan 2012	*Ms Martin and Mr Jones began a relationship after meeting on her 30th birthday.*
02.07.2012	Jeremy Martin born.
Aug 2013 approx.	*Ms Martin and Mr Jones separated, after fighting shortly after Jeremy's 1st birthday. She says he hit her before leaving.*

Date	Information
05.09.2013	Referral from police to social care after Ms Martin (who police thought was depressed) was stopped for drink-driving with Jeremy (14mths) in the car. No further action taken.
Nov 2015 approx.	**Ms Martin says she got back together with Mr Jones around this time, although they continued to argue.**
03.12.2015	Referral from police after Ms Martin called them to her home, asking them to remove Mr Jones, her partner, from her address. No further allegations made, no further action.
18.04.2016 (this referral)	Referral from police after a fight between Jeremy's parents Mr Jones and Ms Martin. Both of them had been drinking. Mr Jones smashed a mirror before leaving.

The following points immediately spring to mind:

- Mr Jones appears not to be Jeremy's biological father, based on the dates given.

- While Ms Martin has had very low times in her life where she has got drunk and felt depressed, these all seem to be triggered by trauma and violence happening around her.

- From September 2013 to November 2015, she seems not to have been with Mr Jones, and there are no known problems during that time. This may suggest she copes well when away from a violent relationship.

None of these points are proved by the chronology, but they are all things I would want to explore in more detail.

This example demonstrates two tips:

1. Include the (approximate) **date of conception** in your chronologies. I started doing this recently and it can be illuminating:
   a) As in this example, it may shed light on paternity (or, alternatively, the dates of the couple's relationship may simply be wrong – check!).
   b) The parents' lifestyle at the time of conception is instructive – if, at the time of a (planned) conception, the couple were fighting and taking drugs (even if they have since stopped), this calls into question their insight into what makes a stable home for a child.
2. Pay as much attention to **gaps** as to events. Periods of stability are as important as periods of dysfunction – you can start asking yourself 'why was this period so bad?' but also 'why was this period so good?'

FOCUSING A CHRONOLOGY ON THE SERVICE USER, NOT THE SERVICE

One of the most common flaws in local authority chronologies is the idea of a 'service-centred chronology', like this:

Date	Information
18.12.2001	Child born.
17.09.2016	Child said her father abused her when she was eight.
18.09.2016	Social Services started s47 investigation.
19.10.2016	Social worker finished assessment.
20.10.2016	Social worker arranged meeting.
22.10.2016	Social worker made referral to CAMHS for child.

When in fact, using the same information and going back into our files, I might come up with something like this:

Date	Information
18.12.2001	Child born.
Approx. 2010	Child said (in 2016) that her father abused her at this time.
18.09.2010	Older sister alleged sexual abuse by father – unsubstantiated.
Mar 2011	School referred child to Social Services due to troubled behaviour.

The key is to **enter events *when they happened***, not when they were first recorded on an organisation's data systems.

Don't just take my word for it: in her damning review of professional failure to prevent child sexual exploitation in Rotherham, Professor Alexis Jay (2014) found both that computerised chronologies were unhelpful (see previous section) and that chronologies weren't as useful as they should be as a result of people entering information when they received it, not when it happened.

This has practical value, analytical value and moral value:

- practical value because it's more 'organised' to have events lined up in the order they took place;

- analytical value because it allows you to start considering causal links and themes; and

• moral value because it reminds us that the service user (be they child or adult) is the person whose story matters here.

The last point is important: too many chronologies are stories of 'what agencies have done' rather than 'the life of this child/adult'. The individual becomes subsumed to the system and to the professional network around them, leading us to miss the salient facts and lose focus.

There is a role for case recording and agency-centred analysis – see the section on **Chronologies versus case notes** for more on this distinction. Agency-centred chronologies and analyses *can* be useful – for example, a senior manager may want to review the effectiveness of their services and how their teams responded to events. Of course, it is then relevant to look at 'how did the agency respond when they received this information?' In this case, the key moments are when the agency received the information. But for most social workers, this kind of quality assurance activity takes up relatively little of their time. The vast majority of the chronologies that social workers write – and all the chronologies that they write as part of a service user's assessment – should be service-user-focused.

There is also a safety implication. The information below is anonymised and fictionalised, but draws on my own experience of different cases. Consider the following chronology extract (I have used days of the week instead of dates, to reinforce the point):

Date	Event
Monday	Mother seen with a black eye and other bruises. She said she fell over at the weekend.
Tuesday	Child taken to doctor due to bruises. Mother said she dropped him at the weekend.
Thursday	Child taken to GP with blood in stool, doctor saw other old bruising.
Friday	Referral to Social Services due to a fight between mother and father.

I have sometimes rewritten chronologies after looking at the information on file. Sometimes I have ended up with something like this, using the same information:

Date	Event
Sunday	*Mother and father had a fight: father hit mother repeatedly while child was in her arms.*
Monday	Mother seen with a black eye and other bruises. Said she fell over at the weekend.
Tuesday	Child taken to doctor due to bruises. Mother said she dropped him at the weekend.
Thursday	Child had blood in stool, doctor saw other old bruising.

The incident on Sunday was reported to Social Services the next Friday. Common practice is to enter this information, as the social worker did for the first chronology, on the date on which it was received. Computer-generated chronologies do the same thing.

Notwithstanding my earlier point about correlation not proving causation, you can see how the sequence of information in the second chronology looks much more concerning than the first chronology. Initially, the chronology shows a fight between parents, following other unrelated information about injuries to mother and child. When the information is presented in the right order, we find ourselves suspecting that the injuries were inflicted by the father.

The chronology is not a bureaucratic tool for audit purposes, which anyone (person or machine) could create, but a key part of the forensic and analytical process needed for any meaningful assessment or investigation.

THINKING BEYOND THE REFERRAL

More than being an agency-centred chronology, a list of 'things that professionals have been involved in' can also end up as a *referral*-centred chronology.

Imagine writing the following chronology entries, *before* you work on a case:

Date	Information
17.09.2015	Anonymous call from a neighbour to say that Mr Ali and Ms Begum shout at each other all day long and they see Ms Begum sitting outside crying at night, saying she wishes she was dead.
27.12.2015	Ms Begum called police to say her husband was hitting her. He was arrested but returned to the home.
08.03.2016	Police called out to parents shouting at each other. Mr Ali said he would be leaving the family home.
14.09.2016 (this referral)	Referral from school to social care. Rashida is playing up in school, biting other children and her parents say they cannot handle her behaviour at home. The school want the parents to attend a parenting class.

Without doing the chronology (or if it's only done as the final action on the case) a social worker might focus on behaviour management and parenting, and fail to address the underlying reasons why Rashida might be misbehaving.

When the information is laid out as above, the theme of fighting in the home is inescapable, and one that a social worker would naturally want to explore further in their assessment. However, I have seen numerous assessments where the only issue explored is the one in the referral – in the example above, Rashida's behaviour – even when there is a substantial history on file.

CONSIDER 'DID THIS MATTER TO THEM?'

Your files may not have a record of the time when a child's mother forgot his birthday because she was drunk, but this might be the stand-out bad memory of his childhood, even in among other events that are 'worse' from the local authority's perspective (seeing his parents fight or use drugs, for example).

The files may also leave out happy moments or reunifications, which also stick in the service user's memory more than in the minds of professionals. Similarly, ask whether a particular meeting had any real significance for the service user, or whether it mattered to them when a professional wrote a report.

CHRONOLOGIES VERSUS CASE NOTES

Many chronologies resemble case recordings. Well-meaning managers, who hope that computers can take chronologies off social workers' hands, also have a case note-based chronology in mind.

You do need to keep good, comprehensive case recordings (see Chapter 4 for more detail) but these are all on file as case recordings – they don't need to be repeated in a chronology.

It isn't a matter of case notes being 'lower-quality' than chronology entries. It depends what you're trying to produce. Good case notes will probably not make useful chronology entries.

This is because of the fundamental differences between the two:

- **When they're entered.** Case notes are entered as-you-go. Chronology entries are entered with the luxury of hindsight. A perfect set of case notes will still only include information known to the social worker at the time.

- **Who they're aimed at.** A chronology is part of the assessment and (in court) part of the bundle. It should therefore be written with judges and service users, as well as other professionals (internal and external to your organisation) in mind.

  This distinction is subtle: anyone can ask to see their social care file, so they'd be able to read any case notes. However, while social workers should always bear this in mind, their primary audience when writing case notes is other professionals within their organisations: their colleagues, their managers and any auditors.

- **What they communicate.** Case notes tell colleagues and auditors you've done your job. They also tell them what's been going on for the service user and their case recently – so your colleague can pick up the case and run with it, with no need to start from scratch.

- **What they are.** Case notes are a running record of actions and information on a case record. Chronologies are a comprehensive, coherent story of a service user, including (but not focused on) their interactions with professionals.

Chronologies tell people what's happened in a service user's life. They highlight what's happened that was significant *to the service user*.

This follows logically from the need to focus a chronology on the service user, not the agency. There is some overlap between the two.

Example A

The day that a vulnerable adult moves into a council care home is both a significant event in terms of case recording (the start of a service, the start of funding for a placement and the start of various professional involvements) and in terms of the person's chronology (a major event in their life when they changed address and started to be cared for). This event would feature in both the chronology and (extensively) in case notes. However, the chronology entry would be much more succinct, while the case notes would include phone numbers, calls, transport arrangements, authorisations, etc.

Example B

A mother tells you that when she was a young child of about seven or eight years old, her father raped her. If she is opening up about this for the first time, the information won't be recorded contemporaneously in case notes, and won't have a specific date – based on her date of birth, you could say roughly what year she's referring to, but couldn't be precise. Nevertheless, this information could be highly significant to a chronology, particularly if the father is still a part of the wider family and especially if he has any foreseeable role in her child's life.

Example C

A social worker is ill who was supposed to arrange a child's therapy session today. Duty social workers and managers have to do considerable work during the day to arrange travel, contact the family and the therapist, and make sure that it still goes ahead. There are numerous case notes on the file reflecting the work done and establishing what arrangements have been put in place. None of this, however, would feature a chronology.

The chronology is the result of professional judgement, not an 'automated' document. In each of the examples above, as with all the excerpts in this chapter, a social worker uses professional judgement in deciding both what to include in the chronology, and how to use it.

Many social workers still confuse chronologies with lists of case notes, but not due to a lack of skill or knowledge. *Fear* may be the issue: social workers can be so afraid of leaving out something important that they take a risk-averse (and exhausting) approach of adding reams of case-note information to the chronology.

This is a real dilemma, and one I sympathise with. Too long, and you'll be criticised for producing rambling documents. Too short, and you'll be criticised for leaving out key information.

But it's not an either/or situation: I encourage social workers to think of a 'pyramid' of information (which we'll return to in Chapter 6) as follows:

THE INFORMATION PYRAMID

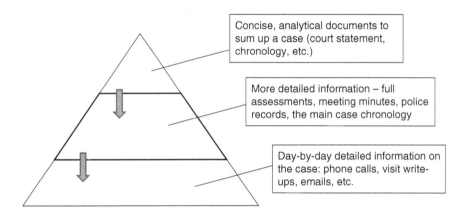

Concise, analytical documents to sum up a case (court statement, chronology, etc.)

More detailed information – full assessments, meeting minutes, police records, the main case chronology

Day-by-day detailed information on the case: phone calls, visit write-ups, emails, etc.

Case notes lie on the bottom 'layer' of the pyramid – a layer that people can 'dip into' if they need detailed contemporaneous records that relate to your chronology entries.

For an example, let's imagine a case involving a suspicious injury to a child, which results in the local authority starting care proceedings. The case notes may look something like this:

Date	Information
21.10.2012	Call from hospital saying baby has multiple fractures. Requested skeletal survey. Made 87A referral to police.
21.10.2012	Strategy meeting at hospital. Police issued police protection.
22.10.2012	Called paediatrician for skeletal survey results. Message left.
22.10.2012	Interviewed both parents.
23.10.2012	Went to court to apply for Emergency Protection Order.

(In reality, the list of case notes covering the same period would be far longer.)

The chronology for the same case, written months later for the final hearing, might read more like this:

Date	Information
20.10.2012	Father threw baby to the floor, causing multiple fractures (admitted in court in March 2013). The next day, mother took baby to hospital, where he was taken into police protection after neither parent could explain his injuries. The local authority initiated care proceedings.

Note three things about the chronology entry:

1. The date. It refers to the time when the father injured the child. This, after all, was the most significant point in time *from the child's point of view*. Being brought into care was significant, and should be reflected too, but always write about events when they happened.
2. The summary. I haven't cut-and-pasted case notes, and I haven't repeated every step in the process. I've given the reader what they need to know – if they want to know more about the local authority's response, they can go down to the next level of the pyramid, and look at reports, or even case notes, for those dates.
3. The use of hindsight. The social worker writing the case notes *couldn't* have included a definitive note of what had happened and when – this only emerged later. But writing with hindsight allows the luxury of including what happened at the time. It makes sense to place this into the chronology using the date when something happened, not using the date when you found out about it.

CHRONOLOGIES FOR THE FAMILY COURT

The formal chronology for the Family Court in a care proceedings case would be subtly different.

Use the raw facts gathered for your chronology, but amend them in two ways:

1. Include a column on 'Significance', summing up why this information matters.
2. Summarise older information into fewer, shorter entries. The courts don't want you to *ignore* information more than two years old, but they do want you to focus (and base your case) on events of the last two years. If a parent had a child taken into care three years ago for the same reasons as you're going into court now, this is clearly relevant – you may find yourself making the case that what has happened recently is not a one-off but a pattern of behaviour, and you'd use historical information as your evidence for this. Your focus, however, would be on what has or hasn't changed since.

Two examples in the same case help make this distinction:

You're making an application for a Care Order in October 2016 for baby Joe, aged nine months. Police found him alone in a home smelling strongly of urine, with multiple injuries of unknown cause. Since then, his mother, Ms Carlos, has cleaned the home up and changed her schedule to ensure he has a childminder at all times.

> **Entry A:** In March 2013, Ms Carlos' older child Carl, aged 2, was placed in the care of his paternal grandmother because Ms Carlos had persistently neglected him, leaving him home alone several times and letting her home become dirty and smelly. She made improvements to the home during these proceedings.

> **Entry B:** In September 2011, Ms Carlos called police to remove her partner Mr Smith from the home, after he had got drunk and hit her. She did not want to give a statement but has had no known contact with Mr Smith since then.

In this example, Entry A should be included in a court chronology, even though it falls outside the two-year guideline. The mother's inability to sustain improvements is clearly demonstrated by her difficulties with her older child. This is relevant to the analysis of the risk of neglect to Joe. Even then, you might sum it up in a single line if possible, telling the court why proceedings occurred and what the outcome was. You wouldn't list every hearing, every incident, etc.

However, you wouldn't include Entry B in the court chronology (although you would keep it in the general chronology on the case file – it would be significant if Mr Smith turns up in future). While domestic violence is a risk to children, this particular incident is not relevant to the care proceedings for Joe. If, however, Mr Smith and Ms Carlos got back together and said this would make things better for Joe, the information would become relevant to the analysis of their relationship (although, again, you would have to demonstrate *current* and future risk rather than simply citing a five-year-old event as evidence of harm).

See the court chronology in the **Examples of chronologies** section below for a more detailed example.

CHAPTER SUMMARY

Your chronology should be:

- The first thing you create (at least in a rough draft) for an assessment.

- Written using professional judgement – you need your skills as a social worker to determine what to include, and to understand its significance.

- A story of events *when they happened*, from the service user's point of view.

- Motivation to read old files, or to find/request them.

- Centred on the service user – their life, their significant events (even if the dates are approximate). *Not* the organisation's list of actions.

- Succinct, and designed to tell a person's (or family's) story. *Not* like case notes – if an auditor or manager wants to check you've done your job, they can look at the notes.

Your chronology should help you:

- Gain a service user's confidence, by showing that you respect them enough to prepare for your visit and save them duplicating the same story again and again.

- Place current events in a historical context (is it a one-off or part of a pattern? Is one type of event usually linked to another?).

- Stay focused on the deeper issues in the person's life, rather than just the presenting issues in the referral.

- Avoid 'start-again syndrome'.

- Save time. Your visits, meetings and reports will be better-informed, so less likely to need repeating.

- Spot trends, and start asking questions about causation (did that happen because of what else happened around the same time?).

- See what's *not* recorded – the long gaps without any (known) incidents of concern are as important as the incidents. Was everything really OK for such a long period? If so, why?

EXAMPLES OF CHRONOLOGIES

Chronology for Joe Bloggs, rough copy prior to visit

Note:

- I would not usually type a rough chronology: in a statutory team I usually wrote this on a notepad to take on a first visit. I have typed this example for ease of reading.

- The right-hand column is 'imaginary' – I would rarely include this in a rough chronology, but it summarises the kind of thoughts I would scribble next to my rough chronology.

For an assessment in September 2016		
Date	**Event**	**(Thoughts)**
05.08.1986	Mother born.	
11.12.1986	Father born.	
12.04.1991	Mother and siblings taken into police protection due to their father severely assaulting their mother. The children had unexplained injuries and were later adopted.	*Mother has grown up in an environment of violence during the early years of her life, which may have affected her preconceptions about relationships and her prosocial skills.*
1997	Mother's grandfather died.	
March 1998	Mother referred to CAMHS after cutting herself.	*This represents self-harming, but note that it followed the death of her grandfather. Was she suffering bereavement or was another factor involved? If bereavement, how has she since developed her coping skills?*
Early 2002	Mother and father began relationship at Pupil Referral Unit.	*Mother and father met after both experiencing troubled childhoods, at the age of only 15.*
June 2003	Father's younger siblings taken into care due to neglect, following a child protection plan.	*Father also experienced neglect, possibly affecting his notions of what represented a normal family life.*
2004 or 2005	Mother later said (in 2004) that when she was 18 father threatened to kill her and they separated for six months before getting back together.	*Threats to kill very serious, but the couple got back together.*
Approx. March 2005	Mother became pregnant.	*Need to clarify precisely when the couple separated: were they together at the time of conception?*
19.05.2005	Drunken fight between parents; police called.	*Role of alcohol in their fights generally? Find police reports and explore more fully.*
12.12.2005	Joe born.	
28.12.2005	Police called to verbal argument at parents' house. Father moved out.	

Jan 2006	Father assaulted mother in front of Joe while collecting his belongings. She reported this (and previous abuse) four weeks later to the police.	
08.03.2006	Social Services completed initial assessment. No further action taken. Mother told the social worker she had improved her relationships with her own birth parents and they were helping her stay safe from father and look after Joe.	*Note that her own parents failed to keep her safe as a child: how have things changed now (if at all)? Are her parents able to provide suitable advice?*
July 2013–March 2014	Child protection plan in place following Joe coming to school dirty. Visits to the home found broken furniture and a poor hygiene. Plan ended after the home environment improved.	*Significance of seven years with no referrals? What was different about this time? When were mother and father together/ separate? Did broken furniture in the home have anything to do with violence (given the history)?*
15.10.2014	Police called to family address – mother alleged father had hit her, then withdrew allegations.	
19.08.2015	Father told his psychiatrist (who referred to social care) that he had thought about killing his family and himself (although not now).	*Note the link to father threatening to kill mother a decade previously: how long have these thoughts been happening? Severe risks involved given actual violence as well as thoughts of killing children.*
14.09.2015	Initial assessment completed – no further action. Analysis found father was not having violent thoughts now, was getting correct help and that both sets of birth grandparents were providing lots of support to mum and dad and Joe.	*How much insight do the grandparents have, given their own history of having children removed from their care due to violence and neglect? Is the 'help' effective?*

15.12.2015	Referral from police – mother said father had beaten her up in front of the children. Initial assessment completed – no further action. Mother said they'd never had any fights before and this was a one-off. Father had been able to stay with his parents for a while, who were very supportive.	*Previous evidence clearly shows this was not a one-off. Mother's denial of any previous violence points to dishonesty.* *How long were parents separated for?*
19.09.2016 (this referral)	Joe excluded from school for fighting with other children, and has been cutting himself.	

Chronology for Joe Bloggs

Note: the amount of analysis under the 'significance' column may vary – it would be legitimate for a social worker to carry out less analysis in the chronology but make these points in their statement instead.

For a court application in November 2016		
Date	**Event**	**Significance**
05.08.1986	Ms Jones born.	
11.12.1986	Mr Bloggs born.	
1991–2003	Mr Bloggs grew up in a very neglected home and Ms Jones with violent parents. Ms Jones and her siblings were all adopted while Mr Bloggs' younger siblings were taken into care. Ms Jones cut herself repeatedly before and after suffering bereavement in 1997, while Mr Bloggs was taking cocaine and cannabis.	Neither parents has the benefit of positive role-modelling in their own birth families. Both sets of birth grandparents are now involved with the family, and our interviews with them find they have no insight into the harm done to Ms Jones and Mr Bloggs. Both parents developed unhealthy coping mechanisms during their teens.
2002–2006	Ms Jones and Mr Bloggs had a relationship beginning at age 15, during which Joe was born. Police investigated three assaults by Mr Bloggs against Ms Jones during this time, and he also threatened to kill	Ms Jones and Mr Bloggs met after both experiencing troubled childhoods. They both admit drinking to excess during their arguments. Mr Bloggs admits he had considered killing Ms Jones.

	her. They also separated around the time of Joe's conception but neither is disputing paternity.	Ms Jones became dependent on her parents in the period after their separation, despite their own history of abuse.
12.12.2005	Joe born	
Late 2006–late 2012	Ms Jones had a six-year relationship with Mr Smith. She left him when Mr Bloggs returned to the area and they reunited. Joe's school says he was sometimes grubby when he started school in 2008 but seemed fairly happy.	No reports of any concerns during this time. Joe says he trusts Mr Smith and wants to see him, although Mr Bloggs forbids this.
2008	Mr Bloggs convicted of causing suffering to an animal and fined	Research[1] shows a link between harm perpetrated on animals and abuse of children.
2013–2014	Social care involved, with a child protection plan in place from July 2013 to March 2014. This was due to Joe's deteriorating hygiene up until mid-2013 (when it started to improve). Joe has since said that his mother and father started fighting again shortly after getting back together, but they told him not to tell anyone.	Joe's account is evidence that violence can occur in the family without us being aware of it, and that they have tried to hide evidence of violence. The parents' resumed relationship seems to have been a trigger for a deterioration in Joe's physical and emotional welfare.
19.08.2015	Mr Bloggs told his psychiatrist (who referred to social care) that he had thought about killing his family and himself (although not now).	Mr Bloggs' persistent thoughts and acts of violence, including thoughts of killing Joe and Ms Jones, significantly raise the risk of physical harm to Joe if he remains at home.
14.09.2015	Initial assessment completed – no further action. Analysis found Mr Bloggs was not having violent thoughts now, was getting correct help, and that both sets of birth grandparents were providing lots of support to Joe and his parents.	On reviewing the case, we do not consider the grandparents protective given their own lack of insight into their own abuse and neglect, and their minimising of the harm done by Mr Bloggs. They have also told Ms Jones not to call the police if he hits her. Mr Bloggs also does not seem to have gained any insights from his psychiatric treatment.

15.12.2015	Referral from police – Ms Jones said Mr Bloggs had beaten her up in front of the children. Initial assessment completed – no further action. Ms Jones said they'd never had any fights before and this was a one-off. Mr Bloggs had been able to stay with his parents for a while, who were very supportive.	Previous evidence clearly shows this was not a one-off. Ms Jones's denial of any previous violence points to a pattern of dishonesty consistent with previous episodes.
Dec 2015 to May 2016	Mr Bloggs and Ms Jones separated.	Again, when the couple are not together Joe has exhibited no signs of concern. Again, however, the couple have reconciled, meaning that we cannot regard their current claim to have separated as a sign of safety for Joe.
June to Oct 2016	Joe's emotional and behavioural welfare deteriorated, including cutting himself, resulting in an exclusion and an assault on another pupil in the PRU. The home was dirty on the first visit, although it improved after words of advice from Social Services. He was taken into foster care under police protection on 14.10.2016 after telling his mentor that his father hits him and tells him he's 'going to beat him till he can't walk'.	Father's acts of violence mean his threats to seriously harm his son are realistic. There is a clear correlation between Joe's periods of disturbed behaviours and his father's time in the family home. While Ms Jones says Mr Bloggs has left the home, we find her claim unreliable given the couple's previous reconciliations. Foster placement used because we do not regard either set of grandparents (both of whom put themselves forward as alternative carers) as reliable or protective. His basic care needs are also unlikely to be met in future: while the home has improved for now, Ms Jones has improved the state of her home on previous occasions only for it to deteriorate.

[1] R. Lockwood and F.R. Ascione (eds.) (1998) *Cruelty to Animals and Interpersonal Violence*, Purdue University Press

REFERENCES

BASW (2014) Show social workers the respect they deserve: Lord Justice Munby, *Professional Social Work*, 11 June 2014

Brandon, M, Belderson, P, Warren, C, Howe, D, Gardner, R, Dodsworth, J and Black, J (2008) *Analysing Child Deaths and Serious Injury Through Abuse and Neglect: What Can We Learn?* Department for Children, Schools and Families

Jay, A (2014) *Independent Inquiry into Child Sexual Exploitation in Rotherham 1997–2013*, Rotherham Metropolitan Council

Munby, J (2013) *View from the President's Chambers (2): The Process of Reform: The Revised Public Law Outline and the Local Authority*, Courts and Tribunals Judiciary

Nelson, D.L., Reed, U.S. and Walling, J.R. (1976) Pictorial superiority effect, *Journal of Experimental Psychology: Human Learning & Memory*, 2, 523–528

Tversky, A. and Kahneman, D. (1973). Availability: a heuristic for judging frequency and probability, *Cognitive Psychology*, 5(1), 207–233

2 Genograms and ecomaps: Knowing the networks

WHAT THIS CHAPTER COVERS

- What genograms are.

- How to make a genogram.

- How to make an ecomap.

- How genograms and ecomaps help your practice.

- Examples of genograms and ecomaps.

Genograms and ecomaps are, like chronologies, a key part of the process of assessment. Like chronologies, they're not just another administrative exercise to delegate or to 'tack-on' to the end of a report. Professional judgement about what to include, and how to interpret it, is as important here as it is for any analysis.

Also like chronologies, genograms (and sometimes ecomaps) are the quick 'visual' that can guide your initial work with the family. Knowing who people are, and where they fit in to the family dynamics, is something you can't afford to skip.

GENOGRAMS: MORE THAN A FAMILY TREE

Family trees have been around as long as there have been families and writing, and draw the map of someone's ancestry. They are concerned with lineage, traditionally to assert social status (e.g., how closely someone was related to royalty, or why they had a 'right' to specific property or land).

Genograms used in social work and medicine are different. First used in the 1960s as a means of 'tracking a presenting problem through the generations' (Bowen 1978), they were popularised in social work practice by the work of Maria McGoldrick and Randy Gerson (1985). Jolley et al. (1980) identified both the usefulness of a genogram (other professionals could absorb, at a glance, key information with a high level of accuracy) and the need for a common set of conventions in creating genograms.

MAKING A GENOGRAM

Different organisations and professions vary in their notations and practices around genograms, but the following principles are widespread and likely to be understood within the social care and clinical professions:

People

Traditionally, each member of the family is depicted by a square for males and a circle for females. A triangle is usually used for a pregnancy but some professionals use it for a person of unknown gender (more often depicted with a question mark). A cross through a symbol indicates that the person is dead.

This binary model fails to take into account gender fluidity. While Hof and Berman (1986) covered issues of gender and sexuality in their seminal article on sexual chronologies, subsequent work (Belous et al. 2012) has recognised this gap. Conventions are still unresolved with regard to gender fluidity. Belous et al. use a square overlapping a circle to denote genderqueer, while using a square or circle to show current gender identity, but noting date of gender transition with M2F or F2M. McGoldrick herself includes a circle within a square to denote female-to-male transitions (and vice versa for male-to-female), and Keith (2012) uses a wide range of symbol combinations to denote sexual attraction, non-monogamy and gender fluidity in families including transgender and intersex symbols.

The challenge is to create a genogram that is both an accurate, inclusive representation of people's lives, and also a straightforward, unambiguous tool for different professionals to read.

Connections

The variety between symbols pales into insignificance compared to the variety of methods used to show people's relationships. Again, the challenge is to produce a system of notation that reflects the diversity of people's lives and circumstances, while also being instantly recognisable to someone else.

The more accepted conventions include a horizontal line to show an intimate relationship (crossed out where the relationship is over) and a vertical line to show a parent–child relationship. Dashed vertical lines usually show an adoption. Traditional genograms differentiated marriages and non-marriage cohabitations: the former shown with a solid line (with two slashes through the line if divorced), the latter with a dashed line (with one slash through the line if separated). Personally I have always treated both types of relationship the same, adding a notation (e.g., 'm. 2009') to show a marriage.

The Wikipedia page on genograms currently shows 20 different connection lines for family relationships and 30 different emotional relationships. It is hard to imagine using more than a few of these 50 connection types in day-to-day practice. If your genogram or ecomap uses more than a handful of familiar connection styles, it might help to include a legend or 'key' for avoidance of doubt.

Households

Common practice (Hartman 1978; McGoldrick and Gerson 1985) is to draw a dotted line around people sharing the same household. For children whose custody is shared between separated parents, two dotted lines might overlap.

Arranging the genogram

You may find yourself with lots of good information and a clear idea of how it fits together into a genogram, but a headache about how to fit it into one diagram. Multiple partners, children from different relationships or other complexities can soon make a genogram 'messy' and unwieldy. In principle, this doesn't matter, but your aim is to make the genogram easy to read, and useful to a reader. At the same time, no one wants to spend their time messing around with textboxes on Microsoft Word when they could be doing something useful for a service user.

As you get more practised at creating genograms, you'll work out a style that suits you and which is easy to create. A few useful conventions to bear in mind:

- Children go left-to-right, in order of age.

- Partners of a central figure go left-to-right in order of when the relationship happened (unless this would make it impossible to include the children in age order).

- Some abbreviations may be proportionate and necessary; for example, a grandparent may have 12 siblings, none of whom are involved in the family, so they can be denoted as '…12 siblings…' to save space.

MAKING AN ECOMAP

There are overlaps between ecomaps (sometimes known as ecograms) and genograms. They both have their roots in a systems theory approach to social work. They both help you explore the wider context of a service user's life, and the networks around them. In some cases, key themes can be shown just as well through a genogram or through an ecomap.

The main differences are that

- The genogram tends to show *family* (biological or otherwise), while the ecomap is broader in scope, including professional and community networks that have significance (positive or negative) in the service user's life.

- An ecomap tends to show the network as it is now (although it may show distant relationships that have previously been close), while the genogram is clearer at showing historical family relationships.

- Genograms lay out the mechanics of people's relationships (niece by adoption, third cousin once removed, etc.) while ecomaps emphasise the qualitative nature of those relationships.

The third difference is a good example of the overlap: a sufficiently detailed ecomap could include complex family relationships in the centre circle; while an advanced genogram could include numerous different lines to demonstrate the nature of particular relationships.

Ecomaps are the creation of Professor Anne Hartman (1978) as part of her systems approach to social work. She wrote:

> **the ecomap is a simple paper-and-pencil simulation [that] maps in a dynamic way the ecological system … Included in the map are the major systems that are part of the family's life … it pictures the important nurturant [sic] or conflict-laden connections between the family and the world. It demonstrates the flow of resources, or the lacks or deprivations.**

The family or individual go in the centre of the ecomap, and the various parts of their network go around them. These parts might be professional services, individuals, families or communities. The links between them (using similar notation to those for genograms) demonstrate the nature of the relationships: how significant and how positive. Short annotations can be useful in explaining the nature of the connections.

The arrows in the ecomap show which direction the effect occurs. If a professional helps a service user, then the arrow would 'point' to the service user. If a family are involved in a dispute then the arrows may go both ways.

HOW A GENOGRAM OR ECOMAP HELPS YOUR PRACTICE

You may find a genogram or ecomap useful at the beginning of your assessment for practical reasons. Just like the chronology, having a rough genogram or ecomap drawn out at the start shows you:

- Areas of confusion or 'gaps' in your knowledge.

- Who might be the most significant people to contact as part of the assessment (tip: the first visit to the service user is a good opportunity to get their details and consent to contact them).

- (Possibly) themes emerging from the nature of different relationships within and around the family.

If nothing else, it reminds you who everyone is! Going on a first visit and realising you can't remember who John Smith is and how he links to the family could be embarrassing. Like the chronology, drawing a rough genogram beforehand can help project competence and make a good first impression.

During your assessment, the ecomap and genogram make useful analytical tools. They provide a starting point for your conversations with the family: a framework for discussing family relationships and family history, and for discussing the nature of important links in their lives. They help focus your thinking on the dynamics around a person, rather than trying to assess the person in isolation.

Hartman's (1978) work provides a useful warning for an age of computerised, segmented assessment tools. She said, 30 years before ICS:

> **If social workers are to avoid reductionism and scientism, if they are to translate a systems orientation into practice, they must learn to 'think systems' or to develop ... new and more complex ways of imprinting reality.**

See **Taking it further**, below, for more on systems theory in social work, and for more on the details and role of these tools in assessment.

Example genogram

This example contains just some of the information potentially included in a genogram. For a rough genogram, scrawled on a notepad to help the assessment, you could also include phone numbers and addresses as a quick memory aid.

The example is far simpler than some of those used by the authors quoted, but shows most of the basic features of a chronology – relationships including adoption and separations, brief labels with key 'red flags', household composition, relevant comments and the suggestion of a theme across generations.

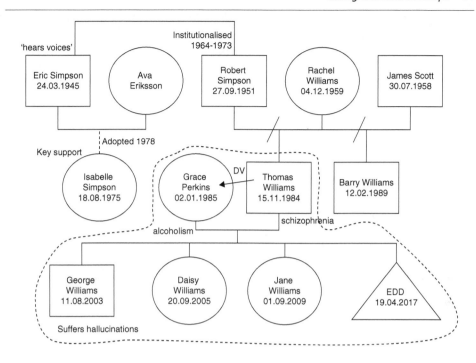

Example ecomaps

The first is a more conventional ecomap. I have used different width lines, but jagged lines to indicate a stressful relationship are also common.

I have used the family from the genogram above for this basic example.

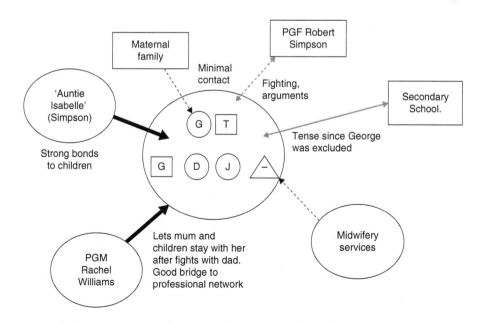

The second might be called a 'hybrid' ecomap/genogram, with elements of both. In this case, the parents are separated and share custody.

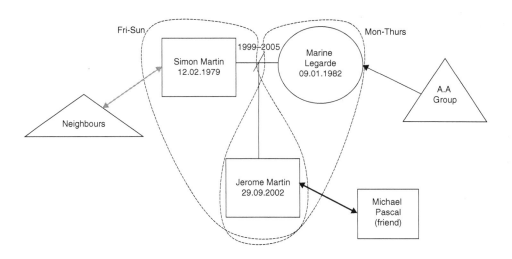

 TAKING IT FURTHER

Advanced use of genograms

McGoldrick, M and Gerson, R (1985) *Genograms in Family Assessment*, Norton

McGoldrick, M, Gerson, R and Petry, S (2008) *Genograms: Assessment and Intervention*, Norton

Systems theory in social work

Gitterman, A and German, C (2008) *The Life Model of Social Work Practice* (3rd edn), Cupola

Helpworth, D, Rooney, R, Rooney, G, Strom-Gottfried, K and Larsen, J (2010) *Direct Social Work Practice: Theory and Skills* (8th edn), Cengage Learning

Merton, R K (1948) *Social Theory and Social Structure*, The Free Press

Case study of the use of genograms to draw out the strengths of African-American families

Chavis, A (2004) Genograms and African American families: employing family strengths of spirituality, religion, and extended family network, *Michigan Family Review*, 9(1), 30–36

Case study of the use of genograms in military families

Weiss, E L, Coll, J E, Gerbauer, J, Smiley, K and Carillo, E (2010) The military genogram: a solution-focused approach for resiliency building in service members and their families, *The Family Journal: Counseling and Therapy for Families and Couples*, 18(4), 395–406

A slideshow on gender variance in genograms – full range of proposed symbols

Keith, C (2012) *Sexual and Gender Diversity Genograms: A Tool to Transcend Hetero-, Cis- and Mono-Normativity in Practice*, www.slideshare.net/SpectraWorkshops/queer-genograms-workshop-poly-conf

REFERENCES

Belous, C, Timm, T, Chee, G and Whitehead, M (2012) Revisiting the sexual genogram, *The American Journal of Family Therapy*, 40, 281–296

Bowen, M (1978) *Family Therapy in Clinical Practice*, Jason Aronson

Hartman, A (1978) Diagrammatic assessment of family relationships, *Social Casework*, 59(8), 465–476

Hof, L and Berman, E (1986) The sexual genogram, *Journal of Marital and Family Therapy*, 12, 39–47

Jolly, W, Froom, J and Rosen, M (1980) The genogram, *The Journal of Family Practice*, 10, 251–255

Keith, C (2012) *Sexual and Gender Diversity Genograms: A Tool to Transcend Hetero-, Cis- and Mono-Normativity in Practice*, www.slideshare.net/SpectraWorkshops/queer-genograms-workshop-poly-conf

McGoldrick, M and Gerson, R (1985) *Genograms in Family Assessment*, Norton

How to get it done: Planning your report in the real world

WHAT THIS CHAPTER COVERS

- The importance of the wider context of your work.

- How your working environment affects your assessments.

- How you might organise the start of an assessment.

- Getting the most out of visits.

- Case recording.

- Deadlines and timeliness.

- Overcoming barriers to getting a report written.

THE CONTEXT OF SOCIAL WORK: IS A GOOD, TIMELY ASSESSMENT EVEN POSSIBLE IN THE CURRENT CLIMATE?

Social workers today are more hard-pressed than ever: between 2008 and 2015, while council budgets were cut by 40 per cent, children's services saw 79 per cent more child protection investigations, 70 per cent more child protection plans and 79 per cent more applications to the courts for Care Orders (Jones, 2015a). Meanwhile, adults' services suffering similar cuts have seen their caseloads rocket after (to name just one pressure) the 'Cheshire West' ruling on deprivations of liberty led to a tenfold increase in DoLS assessments, overloading the system (Law Commission 2015).

The cuts are only part of the story. The nature of social work provision in the UK is changing. Teams, services and whole council departments have been outsourced to private companies in recent years, despite research findings (Stanley et al. 2012) that pilot schemes have decidedly mixed outcomes for young people, and despite intense resistance within the profession (Department for Education 2014). This is part of a wider trend of unprecedented, politically motivated (rather than evidence-based) marketization of the sector – a topic that Ferguson (2008), Jones (2015b) and others address in much greater depth, highlighting the distorting effect of the profit motive on professional judgement, and the damaging impact on accountability, professional judgement and, ultimately, service user welfare.

You may find yourself working as a social worker in a team without statutory control or oversight – this should not be a reason to abandon social work principles, but more reason than ever to focus on the skills and values that make the profession so important. Social workers in the public sector have long had to stand up for their professional values in the face of budget constraints and the 'audit culture' (Munro 2004) of new public management theory, but those in outsourced services will also have to assert their values ahead of the profit motive of their employers. Buchanan et al. (2012) found that only 9 per cent of adult social care workers now worked for a local authority employer.

See **Taking it further** for more links to campaigning organisations to help you add your voice to the debate on social work at a national level.

There is no such thing as 'keeping out of politics' when you intervene in families for a living. Saying that you 'don't have political views' *is* a political view: it simply means you've chosen to accept the status quo and its underlying assumptions about the aims of your work. The history of professional intervention in private life, by people who believed they were doing the right thing, is frequently horrifying. In the future, people will look back on some of what we do now and wonder why we didn't realise it was wrong. It's not only *acceptable* for a social worker to challenge unethical practice and procedures, it's a requirement of our code of conduct (HCPC 2016) and a moral imperative.

This chapter is a small contribution to helping you stay focused on your assessment: how to develop a meaningful, professional understanding of a complex person or family. It looks at how to get your assessment done, even within the time pressures and complications that social work involves.

'DISCLAIMER'

First of all, don't follow my advice.

I don't want you to practice like me, I want you to practice like you. More than being ignored, I'm afraid someone might turn my advice into a rigid and dogmatic system of practice.

Even I don't follow my advice absolutely. Today I practice differently (and I hope better) than I did a year ago. A year from now, I hope to work better than I do today. If anyone had told me years ago that I had to work in a fixed way, I wouldn't have developed the strategies I have now.

Within safe, sensible bounds, experimentation and adaptation is always good for practice.

My practice is influenced by Kolb's experiential learning cycle of concrete experience, reflective observation, abstract conceptualisation and active experimentation (Kolb et al. 1974). Everything I do is subject to a continual process of review, both internally (the reflective part) and externally (where I bring in outside influences) before trying it again. This learning cycle is incompatible with a rigid, dogmatic approach. Certain core principles remain, and any changes are usually small and incremental rather than dramatic and risky, but the process of continual development is essential.

So the advice in this chapter is designed as part of your own process of development. We all have a toolbox of professional skills, much of it similar (since we're doing similar jobs) but all slightly different.

Please don't read this chapter as 'this is how to practice' but as 'this is how I practice'. I've outlined a series of tools that I hope you find useful.

Some of this chapter will seem blindingly obvious, but everything that follows is based on what I wish I'd known when I started, and what I wish every social worker knew.

CREATING THE FOUNDATIONS FOR GOOD ASSESSMENTS

Staying healthy

It's none of my business (or your managers') how healthy you are. However, I couldn't write a book on writing assessments without mentioning health. It's the single most important factor that affects the quality of my work. My best work is done when I'm eating, exercising and sleeping properly.

When you're healthier, you feel better, you'll work quicker and you'll do better work. Research consistently finds the same link between physical health and performance at work: Hogan et al. (2013); Pronk et al. (2004); Fox (1999); Donoghue (1977). And yet many social workers skip breakfast, skip lunch, skip exercise, work all night and/or eat food with a high glycaemic index (GI).

Too many social workers try to do high-quality work with little or no food, or with high-sugar, high-GI food that creates a 'spike-and-crash' pattern of sugar highs and lows. Trying to think clearly with energy levels shooting up and down is an uphill battle.

Your general health is none of my business. I'm only concerned about the effects on social work practice. Stable energy levels:

* allow you to think more clearly when doing complex analysis, so your reports should be better, and

- set you up better for a long or difficult visit – it's no fun being in someone's living room feeling hungry or light-headed and needing to have a challenging conversation that requires your full focus.

Staying organised

To do good social work, it is not enough just to be organised. It is, however, essential to be organised. Your interpersonal and analytical skills are only effective if you manage to go on visits.

Let's start with *emails*. Research (Simon 2015) found workers across different professions average 100 emails per day. Social workers receive (and send) a lot of emails. I've found that:

1. **Emails *are* useful.** They can be copied and pasted into case notes (rather than written down and typed up); they don't require two people to be available for a conversation at the same time; and they provide a clear 'paper trail'. Emails are more accountable and they're more efficient. Face-to-face or voice conversations are vital, but email works well for practical arrangements or where specifics are important.
2. **Emails don't go away by themselves.** The 'ever-expanding inbox' creates risks that people miss the next, crucial message. I've adopted the habit of reading each email when I first see it, and deciding there-and-then whether:
   a) it's irrelevant (in which case delete it);
   b) it's something I need to deal with (in which case deal with it); or
   c) it may be useful for reference another time (in which case use the email server's folder system to file it away).
   Ideally, following this rule keeps an inbox more-or-less clean. This isn't (just) an obsessive habit: every new email now stands out.
3. **Emails can monopolise everyone.** Be empathetic to your colleagues: remember how it feels to get long, pointless or repetitive emails and don't inflict this on others (I admit to doing this far too often). Only 'reply' rather than 'reply to all' unless necessary; if you have an important point to make, make it in a short email (or in person) rather than hiding it the middle of a huge message; and always consider whether a long email is really necessary.

Create a *filing system* – you probably won't have paper files any more, but a few minutes creating folder systems on your personal hard drive and on your email server is time well spent. Most workers I've met save all their documents to just one or two folders. After a couple of years they have several hundred ambiguously named files in the same place, and a hard job locating a key document.

Make the most of *mobile technology*. Whenever you call someone, use your work mobile if possible, and save the number to the contact list. This saves a lot of your time and other people's later, as you're less likely to phone the office in a panic asking for a service user's phone number. Load in any emergency numbers as well – you never know when you'll be in a difficult situation at 6pm and need to call your manager's mobile or the out-of-hours team.

Use the *navigation* app on your smartphone – just as you can load phone numbers into your phone, you can load in locations (for confidentiality, don't label personal addresses with anything that someone else could use to identify them – always imagine your phone could be stolen).

Keep a *calendar*. Until recently I used a paper diary; I've since become an online calendar obsessive – everyone will have a preference. The same confidentiality rules apply: keep only as much information on anything portable as you'd want someone to see if they stole it. An up-to-date calendar/diary is also vital (and usually a requirement of your employer) for safety reasons.

Look after your *workspace*. Wherever you end up sitting, the quality of your working environment makes a big difference to what you can get done. Research (Chae and Zhu 2013) found people could concentrate on one task for 50 per cent longer at a tidy desk compared to a slightly cluttered desk. I take the same approach to papers as I do to emails (and since many employers operate 'clear desk policies', you may not have a choice in this): either it's irrelevant (shred it), something I need to deal with (deal with it) or something I need for reference (scan it and file it electronically).

This is an uncomfortable point to make, since it sounds too close to a corporate obsession with clean, empty spaces. There's a difference between a soulless, homogenised workspace and a tidy workspace that helps *you* work. A tidy workspace will look different for everyone: if I sat at someone else's desk, I might find it distracting, but when they sat at it, they'd know the significance of every object and paper, and know that it was in order. If, however, their workspace felt just as chaotic to them as it looked to me, then this would still hinder their work.

Consider a formal *assessment plan*. Rigid pro forma documents and checklists can hamper, not improve, your thinking, but in the early part of your career a reminder of key tasks might be useful – over time these things will become second nature and you may rely less on a default schedule. Every assessment is different and so every assessment plan ought to be subtly different, although some features – such as checking old files, meeting the key people and doing checks with other professionals – will be almost universal.

Staying on top of casework

You don't need to use *my* system, but you need *a* system. The number of service users you'll work with and the length of time you'll work with them will vary according to the team you're in and what the service user needs. However, in most teams you'll need a methodical system to keep track of what you need to do.

ISN'T THIS TOO TASK-FOCUSED? WHAT ABOUT THE REAL SOCIAL WORK?

This chapter is shamelessly task-oriented, but this shouldn't be how you approach your work as a whole. Far from being reductionist, my practice involves organising everything as efficiently as possible, not because this is what social work is about, but because it frees up space for the real social work to happen. If you've done all your administrative work quickly, this frees up your time for face-to-face work, reflection, and thinking about solving people's problems. This is what your organisational skills are for: tidying the less important tasks away so you can focus on what matters. In my experience, the people who are the most efficient at their paperwork also spend the *most* time face-to-face with service users – a report is easier to write when you know the people involved.

In a front-door service, where I'd work with an average of four new families per week, I found a spreadsheet the most effective way to keep track. I created rows for each family, and my column headings included 'time since allocation', 'time until report deadline', 'time since I saw them' (these allow automatic calculations: the spreadsheets works out for you how many days/weeks you've been working with them), system ID number, whether I've carried out checks, whether my report has been signed off and a longer column with key to-do tasks.

Taking it a bit further, using 'conditional formatting' allowed the various boxes to go green/yellow/red by themselves as time went by. I could see in one screen a quantitative (although not qualitative) summary of my caseload. Another advantage was that I could send it to my manager ahead of each supervision. This never took me much time to maintain, and saved me a lot of time whenever a manager had a question about a case.

This wouldn't be the same system I'd use for a different kind of team, and everyone will have different methods they find effective.

See the section on **Deadlines** regarding timeliness.

Some social workers stand out as particularly productive, good at working with people and good at understanding them. These 'star' workers frequently complain:

> **Everything's a nightmare! I've got too much to do: I have a report to finish tomorrow, I was supposed to call this person yesterday and I'm only doing it this afternoon, and I've still got three visits to arrange for next week and two deadlines coming up. Aargh!**

These are the people who stood out as the most efficient *and* most effective social workers in their departments. The key point of their angst was: *they knew.* They knew what they were behind on, they knew what they had to do, they knew when their deadlines were. They'd sometimes be ahead, sometimes behind. But they'd always know how ahead or behind they were. By contrast, the workers who were struggling would never know what they had to do and when.

STARTING YOUR ASSESSMENT

Your manager says: 'I've got a new case for you – Mr Sanchez. I want you to do a short assessment of him by next week. Here's the referral, see what you can do.'

Next steps: chronology (see Chapter 2) and genogram/ecomap (see Chapter 3). Now you know as much about Mr Sanchez as you can from the paperwork. You've found that there are old files that aren't on your system, so you send an email to your archives department asking for those to be delivered.

SAVING TIME BY WORKING IN PARALLEL: DO YOUR REQUESTS FOR INFORMATION *EARLY*

You'll waste time if you do all your work, then realise there's a 'hole' in your assessment because you need information from agency X. If you've taken three weeks to get to the end of your report, then they take another three weeks to get you the information, the whole exercise takes six weeks when it could have taken three.

Instead, if you contact agency X around the start, then they still take three weeks and you still take three weeks, but you've just halved the time taken for the report, with no extra work by anyone. The same principle applies to parallel planning for children in care, and many other areas of practice.

This is a good time to go back to your manager and clear up expectations. Having read the files first, you're better-placed to ask 'what exactly do you think I should focus on?' *Know why you're doing the assessment.* Your manager may want to know if your team should provide a service, and has a panel deadline coming up. Your department may have a legal responsibility to carry out a specific assessment within a set deadline. You may be worried about a particular risk. Usually this will be obvious from the referral and from your manager's initial instructions. Asking for guidance is important, but more effective when you've done your reading first.

The next useful person to contact will usually be the referrer. Creating your rough chronology and genogram may have shown you gaps in your knowledge, and the referrer could help you fill those gaps. Some of their concern might have been lost between their original contact and the referral document – talking to them is a good opportunity to make sure you haven't missed anything. The referrer can also be a useful source of contact details.

Work out who you need to call, and *call them*. Plan your phone calls just as you would a visit. Know what you're going to ask them, rather than just asking 'do you have any concerns?' etc. Be specific.

If you're likely to be working with the service user beyond the assessment, this is a good time to start creating an email list of the key professionals – this saves time later when arranging meetings or sending alerts.

VISITS

Writing the chronology and genogram, and reading the files in the process, will help you produce a list of questions. This should be flexible – your visit should not be a bureaucratic, question-and-answer session but a flowing conversation, based on what's important. Your list of questions should be a 'crib sheet' rather than a structure for the conversation. Things will emerge during your visits that require a different line of thought: this is where your skill and experience as a social worker comes into its own. This book addresses the practical side of setting up visits. For guides to interviewing services users, see **Taking it further**.

Building this set of questions will save time. Otherwise you'll end up doing more visits than you planned, just because you didn't ask an important question the first time.

Back in the office, you're now ready to meet Mr Sanchez. Seeing him face-to-face will be crucial to your assessment and to any work you do with him. This is where most of your skills as a social worker will be applied.

However, you also need to work out who else to speak to. If he's in hospital, is there a consultant taking care of him? If so, when does the consultant come on shift and when would she be able to speak to you? If his sister is his main carer (and the referral advises making first contact with her), is she in the hospital now? If not, when does she usually visit?

Again, even doing the same amount of real work, there's a lot of scope for saving or wasting time.

Compare these two scenarios (they both assume that you have permission to speak to all the people involved – check this before making contact):

Scenario 1

You rush out at 11am. However, when you get to the hospital, you discover he's having a procedure carried out, so you can't speak to him yet. His consultant is busy on another ward, and his sister has just left.

You have to wait until 1pm to speak to his consultant, who soon has to go on another ward round. You see Mr Sanchez at 1:30pm but he's confused about why you're here. He's upset by the time his sister arrives at 3pm, and she shouts at you for upsetting him and won't talk to you further.

You leave the hospital at 4pm after five hours, having had one brief conversation with the consultant and two tense conversations with Mr Sanchez and his sister. You're very hungry and you know you still need to contact archives and the home support worker.

Scenario 2

You get a phone number for Mr Sanchez's sister from the referrer, and call to introduce yourself and find out if she's at the hospital. She says she's just left as her brother's having a minor procedure, and she needs to do some chores at home, but that's only ten minutes from the hospital so she could see you at home before she goes into the hospital later. You check with the hospital and find out the consultant won't be free until 1pm. You call his sister back and she says she'll have done her chores by 12, so you agree to come round then.

In the extra time, you eat an early lunch and go through the case file in more detail. You contact Mr Sanchez's home support worker who says they're busy but they'll email you a summary of their involvement tomorrow. You also request the old files.

You visit Mr Sanchez's sister at 12. You get to see the home and get some insight into how he lives. Your conversation is friendly and helpful. She says she'll need to introduce you to Mr Sanchez so that he'll be more comfortable (note: there will be other cases where contacting a carer first is not advisable). You agree that you'll go to meet the consultant for 1pm, and she'll follow later.

You meet the consultant at 1pm – she's made time to speak to you so you have a useful meeting. Mr Sanchez is ready to speak to you at 1:30pm, by which time his sister has arrived and introduces you to him. You have a good first meeting with him, both with and without his sister present.

You leave the hospital at 3:30pm, having started to develop a good relationship with Mr Sanchez and his sister, and having had good conversations with both of them, and the consultant, seen the family home, eaten a proper lunch and made your requests from other professionals.

Even if the second scenario seems convenient, it's realistic.

The point of these scenarios is to break the connection between 'being at work' and 'doing something useful'. In the second scenario, you've spent *less* time 'at work', but achieved a lot more and spent hours in direct face-to-face contact with key people, rather than the brief and awkward exchanges you've had in the first scenario. The difference between the two is not your underlying skills or personality, but the planning and communication that went into it. If you experienced the first scenario, you might argue that you 'didn't have time to call lots of people and make plans'. Hopefully the examples show why this is a false notion: the time spent making calls in the second scenario means you spent less time 'working' and yet spent more than twice as much face-to-face time, of a much better quality.

The scenarios also show the importance of *geographical awareness*. Once you know who you have to meet and where, you can start looking up the addresses. It will become obvious to you which addresses are close together, and which ones are close to other locations you need to visit.

Using online maps can save you countless hours, without cutting any corners. Once you know you have three visits in the same local area, you can start exploring when people will be home, and whether you can see them all on the same day rather than make the same round trip three times.

A word of caution: it's all very well being super-efficient and planning a series of consecutive visits, but remember to allow time for visits to overrun, or for you to gather your thoughts afterwards, especially if the visits relate to different cases. Arranging visits one after another works best:

- On a second or subsequent 'non-crisis' visit, where the course of the visit is (although not entirely predictable) at least more predictable than a first or crisis visit.

- Either side of lunch: if my first visit over-runs, it runs into my break rather than into another visit (another advantage to bringing a healthy packed lunch).

- When the visit is planned and reliable: an unannounced visit could be less predictable, or the person may not be there, leaving you at a loose end. Similarly if the person is coming back from the school run, for example, the visit may start late.

- With reasonable time allowed to get from one visit to another, and to have a rest in-between.

Whether you travel by public transport or car, *know your journey times*. Many social workers believe in faster-than-light travel: they believe that a 2pm visit means leaving the office at 2pm and trying to work out the route on the way. Planning your travel is vital, not just to give the service user a good impression but also to focus your mind, allowing you to prepare mentally for the visit rather than trying to work out the route as you go. Again, taking care of the organisational/administrative side of the job frees-up the time to focus on the 'real' work.

You'll also need to consider *who else to visit*. Mehrabian (1972)'s research on communication found that 58 per cent of everything we take from contact comes from *body language*. If you want the full picture, a face-to-face visit is much more useful than a phone call. Depending on the circumstances, you may find that emails/calls are sufficient for professional feedback, but for personal insights from relatives and friends then only a face-to-face meeting will help you understand the situation.

Picture the visit, the setting and how long it's likely to take. The last one will get easier to gauge with experience, although it'll always be educated guesswork. Always allow more time than you think you need – it gives the wrong impression if you have to rush off abruptly.

Consider the *venue*: normally you'll need to see a service user's home anyway, but consider the aims of each visit. If you particularly need to find out someone's views, without pressure from their family, then a 'neutral' venue such as a school or community centre might be more suitable. If you're worried about a home being dirty, then you might find an unannounced home visit more useful.

MAKING A VISIT HAPPEN

What if they don't show up? Sometimes the very nature of the case means the person you want to see is unreliable and forgets or ignores appointments – although never forget that social workers do this too.

There's no way to guarantee a visit will happen. However, you can improve your chances of a visit going ahead:

Communicate

If you need to see someone urgently, then sending out a letter giving an appointment date for 1–2 weeks' time sends the wrong message.

Put yourself in the other person's shoes: how would you feel if a social worker wrote to you saying they were going to see you in a week, not saying why?

Always try to speak to someone on the phone to arrange to meet. This also gives you the opportunity to (briefly) outline what it's about – that may reduce their anxiety. You're more likely to arrange a successful visit by mutual agreement than by imposing a time. It's anti-social to send appointment letters for 'urgent' visits a week in the future, for the middle of the day, to someone who works. Service users frequently complain about lost earnings due to meeting social workers. Some give-and-take will be required, but you may find an 8am or 5pm meeting (if safe) works out better.

You could then send them a text message saying 'I will visit you at [time] on [day]. I look forward to seeing you then. [name]' Immediately they have your work phone number, your name and the appointment time if they forget. All for very little work on your part.

Be creative

Try to think outside the box. I've met people in (quiet) parks, in a private room near their work, at their children's schools or at another family member's home.

Make sure what you're doing is:

- legal;

- proportionate to the need to speak to them;

- fair and respectful.

Within those considerations, remember why you're doing it. Either you need to speak to a person in order to help ensure someone else's safety and well-being (in which case you need to be proactive at locating them) or you don't (in which case should you really be trying to speak to them at all?).

Be honest

Ferguson (2011) called it the 'quiet knock': when a social worker knocks lightly on a door, then scurries away, feeling that they 'tried' to see the family. This isn't OK. Don't break the door down, but remember why you're there. Also, you've already travelled to the address and you're going to travel back again – don't waste that time. Never give up on a prearranged visit for at least ten minutes. During that time, you could try any phone numbers you have for them, and the time allows for the unexpected (they may have gone out to the shops briefly or got stuck in traffic on the way home). Occasionally, persistence can be crucial – I once knocked on doors and windows on-and-off for nearly 20 minutes before a young child came to the door and said 'mummy's really ill...'

Be on time

Being late for visits is unfair: in children's services, parents are criticised for being late to school or late to meetings, and many services record that a service user 'did not attend' if they're late by 15 minutes. Lateness also gives the wrong impression: if you're on time, they know that the visit matters, and that *they* matter, to you.

CASE RECORDING

Don't focus on the administration, but incorporate it into your practice in such a way that it becomes at worst 'background', and at best a way of helping you do the work that matters.

Only write everything once

On the phone

Some people use a pen and paper to write notes from their telephone conversation. Then they hang up, and start typing up the notes into the system. That takes twice the time, for no extra benefit.

You free up a lot more time if you type as you talk. Not everyone can touch-type, but still fewer people can take shorthand: so whether you're typing or writing, either way you won't necessarily get everything verbatim. Typing while you're on the phone is no more distracting than writing down an accurate record at the same time, and halves the times taken up by phone calls. You don't even have to type into the database – any word-processing screen will do, and copying-and-pasting into the database later is quicker than transcribing your notes.

Within written documents

Starting with case notes, you might be tempted to either:

1. Copy-and-paste blocks of text from one document to another, or even within the same document.
2. Paraphrase, so you write a slightly amended version of the same thing in one section after another (usually to avoid doing number 1).

Both of these are aggravating to read, and number 2 can waste a lot of your time.

Copying-and-pasting within the same document verges on bullying the reader: why make them trawl through the same text over and over? Remember: *write so it can be read, not so it can be written.* You're not trying to tick a box by finishing a task, you're trying to communicate your understanding to another person.

Standard documents are designed for a variety of situations. So the headings may not apply precisely to your case. If you haven't got anything relevant to say in a particular box, don't say anything. Or if you've already addressed it in a previous section, say 'see section B4', etc. There is no purpose in someone reading the same text more than once in the same document.

Copying between documents is more complicated: the reader of document A may not have access to document B, so when can you cross-reference and when do you have to repeat yourself?

As with so many 'administrative' tasks, professional judgement is needed. Who's reading the document, and what other papers do they have access to? For court, the relevant documents are all in a court bundle and you need only cross-reference the document required.

Is the document you're writing the 'primary document' that people will look at for the topic in question? For example, if you're writing the main assessment of someone's needs, then it makes sense to include information about their needs in detail. Whereas if you're writing a supporting document about another family member who helps that person, then it makes sense to refer to your main assessment regarding the service user's needs, and provide more detail about the family member in the supporting document.

Both copying-and-pasting and paraphrasing should be kept to a minimum. The courts want shorter, more analytical evidence, not repeated blocks of text. But…

Write case notes as though they're going into a report

Case notes will rarely be read by other professionals or a judge (although they *could be*, so write them accordingly). But when working for statutory teams, I spent the majority of my 'office time' writing case notes. This saved me a lot of time and ensured better records. I eventually developed a habit of writing up my case notes immediately, in a format that fit smoothly into the report I was working on.

For example, whereas originally I might have written:

> **Spoke to Jane Collins, deputy head at St John's High School. Said Jim is good at school with no major issues. Said does plays, poetry, sports etc., expected Bs, Cs all subjects. No SEN, etc. Regular attender 98 per cent**

I ended up writing the same note like this:

> **Education**
>
> **Jim is in Year 10 at St. John's High School, Newton. His deputy head teacher, Ms Collins, told me that he is an above-average student, predicted to achieve B and C grades in all subjects. He has no known special needs and Ms Collins described him as a 'very good student, the kids like him and he has some good friends. He plays lots of sports and he's quite creative: he really enjoys acting and writing poetry, and set up a poetry club that a lot of children joined.' Jim's commitment to his education is evidenced by his attendance of 98 per cent this year.**

The second note took longer to write. But it's more useful: it contains the direct words of the person I spoke to (more on direct quotes in Chapter 5); and I could copy-and-paste this into a section on education in an assessment report.

This becomes easier as you become more familiar with your report structure, although see Chapters 5 and 6 regarding the importance of letting the assessment guide the structure, not the other way around.

Copying from case notes is the one time I'd recommend copy-and-pasting, yet the one most underused. Otherwise you might find yourself writing about the same conversation in a case note, in a report and then in a court statement, a slightly different way each time.

This seems minor, even petty, but multiplied by several hundred case notes this frees up a lot of precious time to do more valuable work.

This doesn't mean your reports are a 'collection of case notes' – you'll edit them and add to them as you complete a report. But it saves you time on the 'information' portions of your report, giving you more time to focus on causation. You can even include draft analytical sections in case notes, for example:

Analytical reflection

Provisional thoughts: The chronology and school feedback suggest a close correlation between times Mr Jones has been out of the family, and times the children have been dirty and hungry in school. The implication may be that Ms Smith struggles to meet the children's basic care needs on her own, and this may be part of her reason for inviting him back into the home despite the violence.

This is in your mind anyway, so why not 'capture' it while you remember? By the time you write your assessment, you may have a different analysis and this case note may be obsolete. However, if your thoughts were correct, then this entry provides more material for your assessment, as well as evidence of your thinking at the time.

If you write your case notes the *same day* (or at the latest the next day) after a visit or conversation, they'll be 'fresher' and more in-depth. You may find that the case notes that you write immediately contain more reflections on what you thought and on body language, sights and smells, etc., rather than just listing what was said.

These tips may sound demanding (and writing up comprehensive notes on the day is a hard discipline to get into) but they turn your case recordings from an additional task into a store of your knowledge of a case. You can then dip into this store for your assessments. It also acts as a running record for any other worker to pick up and work with, if required.

DEADLINES

'Timescales' – one of social workers' biggest frustrations, right up there with 'recordings', 'hot desking' and 'restructuring'. So how do you navigate this particular minefield? How do you balance quality with speed?

More speed, less haste

The last question can be a false trade-off. No social worker produces a good assessment in ten minutes – there's no getting round the need for a certain amount of focused, reflective time if your analysis is going to be any good. But beyond a certain point (a point that will vary case-by-case), the law of diminishing returns applies: spending ten hours on an assessment will probably produce a better piece of work than spending five hours on it, but will spending 50 hours create something five times as good? Again, it depends on the depth and complexity of the assessment you need to do, but the quality won't keep improving for every extra minute spent on the work.

From my experience, the social workers taking *longest* to get their work done are *not* producing the highest-quality work – far from it. I also found the social workers doing the quickest assessments were spending *more* time face-to-face with families.

Within reason, a quicker report allows more 'momentum': when doing a visit, you've still got the themes from the previous visit fresh in your mind. You'll need a balance – time to reflect after each contact is important – but spending weeks or even months between appointments is unlikely to produce better understanding.

Also, getting something done quicker helps your mental health. Research (Tice and Baumeister 1997) finds putting off a task results in lower-quality work and higher overall stress levels. So if you work promptly, your work is better *and* you feel better.

Timeliness, not timescales

So while working quicker can mean better quality, and while people shouldn't be 'left hanging' for longer than necessary, the culture of timescales has come to obsess social work. The culture grew all-consuming in the 2000s, culminating in a fixation on meeting time targets.

This situation was improved somewhat after Eileen Munro's (2011) review of child protection. Her first recommendation included the replacement of rigid timescales with those created using professional judgement – a social worker should consider for each assessment how much time should be allowed – while her fourth recommendation was that 'performance information' (including timescales) should not be used as the key measure of how well a service was working.

However, the fixation with arbitrary deadlines casts a long shadow, and in children's services the preoccupation with assessment timescales has been replaced by the requirements of the public law outline (Ministry of Justice 2014) to conclude proceedings within six months.

In practice, the only 'timescale' that matters is '*how quickly does this child/adult need me to do this?*' This will vary by case, and is meant to be a professional judgement.

Sometimes a person's needs will be met as long as the assessment is done within a month. Sometimes the situation demands that you do it in two days. Sometimes, in a duty emergency, you may need to analyse information and come to a decision (albeit without doing all the paperwork immediately) within a few hours.

You may find these strategies useful when trying to achieve timeliness (rather than timescales):

Count up, don't count down

One of my biggest objections to arbitrary deadlines is they make things take *longer*. If a vulnerable adult might be suffering abuse from his own family, then which of these creates more urgency:

- being told 'you have another ten working days to complete your investigation', or

- knowing that you have been this person's social worker for two weeks while they might be suffering abuse?

I find the 'counting-up' approach more effective. Asking 'how long has this awful situation been going on?' strikes more of a nerve than asking 'how long do you have until your arbitrary deadline for this investigation?' The latter makes it feel like a bureaucratic process you have to complete; the former keeps you focused on the welfare of the person involved.

For that reason, when I had a 'case tracker' (see **Creating the foundations for good assessments: staying organised**), the main automated timer involved a clock counting *up* for how long I'd been allocated to each child, not the deadline for the assessment.

Set your own deadlines

A deadline focuses our minds. But arbitrary deadlines cause delay because your mind drifts to the deadline date. If I tell you 'get this report written by 10 March', already you're picturing yourself completing the report around 8–10 March. This may bear little relation to the time the report actually takes.

If a deadline falls on 10 March, you may finish sometime between 8 and 11 March. So *set your own deadlines*. If you're told that a report has to be in by 10 March, record the deadline as 25 February. The same mental process takes place – you'll probably either just meet, or just miss, the 'deadline', but it'll be your 25 February deadline. This amounts to a shifting of a valuable resource: the natural 'surge' in activity and focus that you experience when you approach the 'real' deadline, relocated to a time well before that deadline.

This doesn't mean rushing. The time you'd be most likely to rush is when you're at the 'real' deadline, with managers on your back demanding the report. Working quickly is not the same as rushing – if you reach *your* deadline and need to incorporate new information or rewrite a section, this is fine: you have two weeks to make changes.

GETTING IT WRITTEN

See Chapter 4 for more on writing style and practice.

This section is about the practicality of 'getting it done'. Many good social workers 'freeze' in the office, finding it hard to start a report, build momentum or bring it to a finish. Most offices are hectic, noisy places – the following techniques, in my experience, help create the space for thinking and writing to happen:

Think outside the box (and the office)

Different people find different times and locations more conducive to good work. Some people are most productive sitting in an office, between the hours of 9am and 5pm precisely. Others aren't. Some do their best work from 7am to lunch; others from mid-afternoon to late at night. You'll develop a sense of when you're most analytical and focused, and when you're most receptive and attentive, and try to arrange your 'writing time' and visits accordingly – you won't always have the option, and you need to develop flexibility, but it helps to 'know yourself' and know when you'll do your best work. For example, if you find you're at your sharpest in the morning, you might reserve the afternoon for administrative tasks, or for your less important meetings, when you get the choice.

Some social workers benefit from working in an office, others prefer to work at home (when possible) or even in their car. Many other professionals or students enjoy working in cafés or other public places, but this carries an inherent data protection risk: even if your hardware is secure, people could look over your shoulder. Cafés and other settings are best used for non-sensitive information, like an essay for university.

Boundaries with colleagues

Try to differentiate between two types of conversations, which seem very similar:

1. The constructive, reflective case discussion that draws on colleagues' wisdom and tries to solve a problem as a team.
2. The long complaint about how stressful and difficult a case is, without looking for a solution.

The first kind are vital – the lifeblood of good teamwork, and a key part of your professional development and practice. The second can drain the energy out of a team, sucking both workers into what Eric Berne (1964) would have called a 'why don't you? yes, but (WDYYB) game' with no positive outcome.

Social workers who are keen to help their colleagues can find themselves drawn into the latter, mistaking them for the former. You can inadvertently trigger one of these conversations as well – when you find yourself talking at length about a case, ask yourself: 'What am I trying to achieve? What do I want to ask this person?' Otherwise you may find yourself duplicating stress, not solving a problem.

If you really need to get a report written and want to (politely) avoid interruptions, I recommend *headphones*: they're less about shutting out all noise (they can only do this to a degree) and more about sending a message: you *can* be spoken to, if necessary, but anyone wanting to speak to you will have to actively tap you on the shoulder and interrupt you. This is harder to do than to casually pull you into a conversation from across the office.

The fear factor

When I started teaching court work skills, I was struck by the differences in how long it took social workers to write a court statement – it wasn't that some were quicker than others (this is to be expected), but that some were *five times* quicker than others. I found no correlation between quality and time taken. This difference seemed to apply regardless of experience, typing speed or caseload.

Eventually I surmised that the 'fear factor' mattered more. Once you've produced a report, you've made something that can be criticised. If you write nothing, you'll be criticised, but in a way you can predict. Creating anything means creating something that other people can attack – accepting this at an emotional level is essential to getting anything done.

It also means writing something that might be *wrong*. Any useful assessment will make statements about what causes what, and about what is likely to happen in the future. These statements might turn out to be untrue. One solution is to write nothing at all. Another is to write a long report that manages to avoid 'sticking your neck out' and committing to a position – too many intelligent workers waste their talents by mastering this kind of fudge. The best solution is to write the best report you can with the information you have and be honest about areas of uncertainty. You're not expected to predict the future, and you're not expected to be right all the time. Writing anything of value means accepting that sometimes *you will be wrong*. The maturity and resilience required to accept this is an often-overlooked part of a social worker's skill set.

USE SUPERVISION

Between your manager asking you to write a report and signing it off, they should be a significant source of wisdom and an active part of the assessment. Your supervisions (both arranged and ad hoc) should be a useful analytical exercise, not a checklist of targets missed or met. Both you and your manager have responsibility for making supervision worthwhile. You should come ready with questions to ask each other, looking to get to grips with a difficult problem rather than just talk about deadlines and performance.

A good relationship with your manager and good supervision habits make a difference.

Your manager will be busy and under pressure, and won't know a case as well as you do. So make life easy for them: prepare a list of questions or the skeleton of a problem you're trying to understand, provide succinct summaries where necessary and ask for a constructive conversation. Giving them something (short) in writing beforehand will allow them time to reflect before you speak. Your manager should be pleased to hear challenging, detailed questions about a case, from someone who's thought about it, and a good manager will rise to the challenge.

CHAPTER SUMMARY

The following are personal strategies that have helped my practice. Some of them you may find obvious, some of them you may find useful and some of them may not work for you. However you work, never treat your practice as 'fixed', however prescriptive your organisation, and always keep reflecting and developing.

General principles:

- 'Front-load' your work: a little time planning saves a lot of work later.

- Stay organised.

- Stay healthy.

- Stay focused: 'what's happening here, and what do I need to do about it?' rather than getting wrapped up in targets.

Starting an assessment and doing visits:

- Start work straightaway. Do a chronology (See Chapter 2) and genogram/ecomap (see Chapter 3).

- Request *early* any information that may take time to come back.

- Work out who you need to talk to (including your manager and the referrer) and talk to them.

- Know why you're doing the visit and plan what questions to ask.

- Be proactive about making a visit happen.

In the office:

- Do write-ups so that they would be suitable for an assessment or other report.

- Only write the same thing once, then cross-reference wherever possible.

- Setting earlier deadlines for yourself creates less pressure and less rushing.

- Count up, not down: think 'how long have I been working on this?' not 'how long before that deadline?'

- Avoid time-wasting arguments and draining conversations.

- Face your fear: any worthwhile assessment involves 'sticking your neck out' and using professional judgement.

 TAKING IT FURTHER

Campaigning organisations

Age UK, www.ageuk.org.uk/get-involved/campaign

British Association of Social Workers, www.basw.co.uk/campaigns (full disclosure: I am a BASW member and have provided training for them)

Community Care, www.communitycare.co.uk/stand-social-work-2015

SCOPE, www.scope.org.uk/campaigns

Social Work Action Network, www.socialworkfuture.org

UNISON, www.unison.org.uk/our-campaigns

News and debate

British Association of Social Workers, www.basw.co.uk/news

Community Care, www.communitycare.co.uk

Guardian Social Care Network, www.theguardian.com/social-care-network

Independent, www.independent.co.uk/topic/SocialWork

Direct work and interviewing tools

Aspinwall-Roberts, E (2012) *Assessments in Social Work with Adults*, Oxford University Press

Community Care (2015) *Tools Social Workers can Use to Talk to Children*, www.communitycare.co.uk/tools-social-workers-can-use-to-talk-to-children

Davies, K and Jones, R (2015) *Skills for Social Work Practice*, Palgrave Macmillan

Koprowska, J (2005) *Communication and Interpersonal Skills in Social Work*, Learning Matters

Tait, A (2012) *Direct Work with Vulnerable Children: Playful Activities and Strategies for Communication*, Jessica Kingsley

REFERENCES

Berne, E (1964) *Games People Play: The Basic Handbook of Transactional Analysis*, Ballantine Books

Buchanan, P, Fenton, W and Woodrow, S (2012) *The State of the Adult Social Care Sector and Workforce in England*, Skills for Care

Chae, B and Zhu, R (2013) Environmental disorder leads to self-regulatory failure, *Journal of Consumer Research*, 40(6), 1203–1218

Department for Education (2014) *Consultation on Powers to Delegate Social Care Functions: Government Response*, Department for Education

Donoghue, S (1977) The correlation between physical fitness, absenteeism and work performance, *Canadian Journal of Public Health*, 68(3), 201–203

Ferguson, H (2011) *Child Protective Practice*, Palgrave Macmillan

Ferguson, I (2008) *Reclaiming Social Work: Challenging Neo-Liberalism and Promoting Social Justice*, Sage

Fox, K (1999) The influence of physical activity on mental well-being, *Public Health Nutrition*, 2(3a), 411–418

HCPC (2016) *Standards of Conduct, Performance and Ethics*, Health and Care Professions Council

Hogan, C, Mata, J and Carstensen, L (2013) Exercise holds immediate benefits for affect and cognition in younger and older adults, *Psychology and Aging*, 28(2), 587–594

Jones, R (2015a) Child protection cases have rocketed – Cameron's only answer is privatisation, *The Guardian*, 15 December

Jones, R (2015b) The end game: the marketisation and privatisation of children's social work and child protection, *Critical Social Policy*, 35(4), 447–469

Kolb, D A, Rubin, I M and McIntyre, J M (1974) *Organizational Psychology: A Book of Readings* (2nd edn) Prentice-Hall

Law Commission (2015) *Impact Assessment no. LAWCOM0044: Mental Capacity and Detention*, Law Commission

Mehrabian, A (1972) *Nonverbal Communication*, Aldine-Atherton

Ministry of Justice (2014) *Practice Direction 12A: Care, Supervision and other Part 4 Proceedings: A Guide to Case Management*, Ministry of Justice

Munro, E (2004) The impact of audit on social work practice, *British Journal of Social Work*, 34(8), 1075–1095

Munro, E (2011) *The Munro Review of Child Protection: Final Report. A Child-Centred System*, The Stationery Office

Pronk, N, Martinson, B, Kessler, R, Beck, A, Simon, G and Wang, P (2004) The association between work performance and physical activity, cardiorespiratory fitness, and obesity, *Journal of Occupational & Environmental Medicine*, 46(1), 19–25

Simon, P (2015) *Message Not Received: Why Business Communication Is Broken and How to Fix It*, Wiley

Stanley, N, Austerberry, H, Bilson, A, Farrelly, N, Hargreaves, K, Hollingworth, K, Hussein, S, Ingold, A, Larkins, C, Manthorpe, J, Ridley, J and Strange, V (2012) *Social Work Practices: Report of the National Evaluation*, Department for Education

Tice, D M and Baumeister, R F (1997) Longitudinal study of procrastination, performance, stress, and health: the costs and benefits of dawdling, *Psychological Science*, 8(6), 454–458

4   **Writing**

'If you can't explain it to a six-year-old, you don't understand it yourself.'

Richard Feynman (attributed)

WHAT THIS CHAPTER COVERS

- The context to your writing.

- Writing style for reports.

- Common dangers to avoid:

    o   The passive voice.
    o   Generic terms for specific events.
    o   Jargon.

- The oppressive power of language.

CONTEXT: THE CHANGING NATURE OF SOCIAL WORK LANGUAGE

Writing is not a neutral act, and the tools and skills you use to write are not just technical. Assessments are the product of the human, the tool(s) used and the environment they're working in. This needs to be understood as a 'combined cognitive system' (originally coined by Nunnally and Bitan 2006 in a healthcare context), not just in terms of its component parts. This concept doesn't remove your responsibility for your work: instead, it requires you to be conscious of the context you're working in, and the effect of your tools and environment.

Since social workers started using prescribed, computerised databases, the 'computer's ontology' (Aas 2004) has not just provided a means of recording words, but has shaped how we write. 'The database is a strong contrast to the narrative' (Aas 2004) – segmented, compartmentalised forms 'break up the flow' of your writing, pushing you towards an atomised, reductionist view of a person. Rasmussen (2000) calls this process a transformation from 'knowledge' to 'information'. The more prescriptive the tool you have to use, the more proactive you have to be to avoid breaking the complex picture of service users' lives into 'compartments'.

We need narratives: they 'provide a sense of coherence and continuity in a person's life; they are the "red threads" connecting the various events and connecting the past, present and the future into a unique (meaningful) entity' (Calhoun 1995).

The environment of the wider profession, as well as the tool, makes a difference to how social workers use language (spoken and written).

Ferguson and Woodward (2009) state: 'On the basis of erroneous claims about efficiency and effectiveness, public sector language was transformed ... terms like "value for money" and "consumers" were bandied about as managerial principles and practices took hold.' See **The dangers of jargon** for more on the choice, and effect, of language.

First I will explore some basic writing principles, and some common flaws in social work writing.

WRITING STYLE

Write so it can be read, not so it can be written.

Don't just write something because you've been told to write it. Write to help another person understand something important.

I recommend Stephen King's *On Writing: A Memoir of the Craft* (2000) as a general guide to writing for an audience. While King is better known as a prolific horror writer than a contributor to social work, he has a skill relevant to social workers (and other professionals): an instinctive 'knack' for keeping a reader's attention.

Authors like King, J.K. Rowling and Terry Pratchett have sold millions of books without using flowery language but because their writing 'flows' and keeps people turning the pages. Good social work writing should be easy to read.

King calls good writing 'real telepathy'. When I write: 'a white cat sat on an oval brown rug', I have shared a mental image with you. This is an essential skill for court work: the judge has never met the service user, so you want to transmit what you've seen and heard into the judge's head. This is best achieved by simple language, concisely written.

Always think about King's 'constant reader': how your document will be read. Will the reader be focused on your elaborate vocabulary and spend time trying to make sense of your sentences? Or will they think about the family you're writing about, starting to understand them in the same way you do?

Your report *will* be read: by service users and professionals, now and in the future. You still need to write about difficult and unpleasant subjects, but you should do so straight-forwardly and sensitively.

Write for fun

Writing a short story is wonderful practice for social work reports. Even though it's nothing to do with social work, writing a story develops three good habits:

1. Making a start.
2. Keeping it short and to-the-point (especially if you write it for children).
3. Finishing it.

Many experienced, skilled social workers struggle with reports because they struggle to do these three things.

Accountability

A common question: 'when should I say "I" and when should I say "we" or "the local authority"?'

Different social workers have different styles. There is no golden rule provided your work is clear and *accountable*. Judges get exasperated by social workers who avoid giving their own professional view, and who hide behind a corporate wall. They will be unlikely to tolerate you saying 'it is the view of the local authority that the mother is unable to protect her children' – they want to know if this is *your* view.

I recommend:

- If you are giving *your* professional judgement on something, or if *you* observed something, say 'I'. You are the expert in the case, and expected to be accountable as such. *You* went into a family home – while you may have been representing a local authority, it was still you who went in.

- If the local authority are proposing a particular placement or package of services, say 'the local authority' (or whoever your organisation is). The provision of services is a corporate decision, so it makes sense for you to use the wider term. However, if part of the care plan is for you to do direct work with a service user, then it will again make sense for you to say 'I will do ...'

- Use the active voice (see next section **The dangers of the passive voice**) – the sentence 'it has been observed that...' is grating and lacks accountability. 'I observed that...' or 'Mr Jones observed that...' works much better.

The personal accountability makes some people uncomfortable: after all, every report has to be signed off by a manager or even a senior manager, and they may ask you to revise what you write, since your report represents the view of the local authority. Judges know this. They can also tell when a social worker is hiding behind the organisation's view instead of giving their own. Stevenson (2014) reports Justice Jack criticising and naming social workers for being 'visibly biased in their attempts to support the local authority's case'. Judges prefer a nuanced and honest view to an unequivocal and dogmatic one, and it gives your overall argument more strength.

What the courts highlight is that the social worker's duties to their profession, the courts and the family outweigh their duty to an employer. If you have sworn an oath to tell the truth in court and are asked for your own view, you are required to give it.

If you don't agree with a particular position, don't write it. Telling your bosses (politely and with evidence) that you disagree with them may be frightening in the short-term, and cause tension, but it's also an ethical requirement of your profession and demonstrates integrity.

The template

You'll often have to write a document that comes with its own boxes to fill in. Don't let this interfere with your thinking. These documents were written for a wide range of cases, not for your case specifically. Within any 'box' don't be afraid to improvise: create your own headings as they fit the 'flow' of your argument. Otherwise you may end up with some very large blocks of text that make it harder to read.

As you gain experience, you'll gain more confidence in doing this. No court has ever criticised a social worker because they haven't filled in Box B6 – they have, however, criticised social workers for not considering an important issue. Your report should be focused on substance, not form, and the structure should fit the person and their situation, not the other way around.

See **Appendix** for guidance on writing the local authority social work evidence template ('the statement') and other documents for the Family Court.

THE DANGERS OF THE PASSIVE VOICE

Bad: 'It has been reported that the children have been neglected.'

Good: 'An anonymous neighbour said that Mr Jones neglected his children by failing to feed them and leaving them home alone every day.'

Subject-verb-object. This basic sentence structure ('Bob told me') works much better than using the passive voice ('I was told').

Yet far too many social workers write passive sentences. This is about more than grammatical pedantry:

You lose accountability

'It is believed that the children are at risk of significant harm': *who* believes it? If you believe it, say so. If their aunt believes it, say: 'The children's aunt, Ms Stevens, believes they are at risk of significant harm.'

The danger is that rumour can pass for evidence, or that prejudice can hide behind vagueness. Saying that *you* consider a carer unsuitable forces you to spell out why and to do so transparently. Saying that 'they are considered unsuitable' fudges the point.

You lose crucial information

'It has been reported that the children were scared and dirty': *who* reported it? If you use the passive voice in your writing, assume that you will be asked this question. Sentences like this can create a trail of confusion: the phrase will be repeated in one report after another, until it ends up in a court report and requires a lot of 'digging' to find the original information.

Munby (2014) complained that:

> **[There are] allegations in relation to the father that 'he appears to have' lied or colluded, that various people have 'stated' or 'reported' things, and that 'there is an allegation'. With all respect to counsel, this form of allegation, which one sees far too often in such documents, is wrong and should never be used ... Failure to understand these principles and to analyse the case accordingly can lead, as here, to the unwelcome realisation that a seemingly impressive case is, in truth, a tottering edifice built on inadequate foundations.**

You lose focus

My best case study comes from the excellent work by Jackson Katz (2003). The following example is adapted from his training:

A simple sentence can evolve like this:

1. 'Steve beats Amy.' This is simple: subject-verb-object. Steve does the beating. We focus on Steve. But it changes to:
2. 'Amy is beaten by Steve.' A passive sentence. Steve is now, as Katz puts it, 'on the end, close to falling off the map of our psychic plain'. The focus is now on Amy, just by moving the words.
3. 'Amy is beaten by *her partner*' (my addition). You'll read this in a lot of reports. Don't tolerate it: call the referrer and find out *who* beat her. It's dangerous when you have several reports over time: is it the same partner? Is it the partner she has now?
4. 'Amy is beaten.' Now you've stopped thinking about a 'beater': the sentence is entirely about Amy, who may never have hurt anyone.
5. 'Amy is a beaten/battered woman.' Subtly, one step at a time, you've travelled from a sentence about Steve beating someone (in this case Amy), to a sentence about Amy

being a battered woman and Steve being non-existent. We are now approaching victim-blaming: the onus is on working with Amy to 'stop her being such a battered woman' rather than punishing the offender and protecting the innocent.

In practice I have seen this with different forms of abuse. I've been asked by managers, reviewing officers and lawyers to 'work with the mother to reduce her risk of being beaten' and, worse, 'try to find out why she keeps getting beaten in different relationships'.

For avoidance of doubt, there *is* important work to be done with survivors of domestic violence: education about the signs of abuse and empowering guidance about putting their own (and their children's) safety first, as well as physical protection such as home security and even a new address. It *is* important to work with the non-abusing parent (Forbes et al. 2003 re: sexual abuse; Featherstone and Peckover 2007 re: domestic violence) for a safety plan to be effective.

However, this is different from moving the focus of violence from the perpetrator to the victim. Simple uses of language can help remind us where responsibility lies.

THE DANGERS OF 'CATEGORIES'

No individual ever 'suffers domestic violence': they get punched, kicked, spat at, stabbed, strangled, scratched and hit with bottles, sticks, etc. 'Domestic violence' describes the horrifying catalogue of millions of individual acts inflicted on millions of individual people. It makes sense to talk about '50 per cent of domestic violence cases' or 'approaches that help protect people from domestic violence'. However, saying 'on 15th May Ms Begum suffered a domestic violence incident from her husband' obscures the reality.

The same applies to other terms: 'substance misuse', 'physical chastisement', 'self-harm', 'sexual abuse', 'neglect', etc. All these terms are useful when talking about the aggregate (e.g. '5,000 sexual abuse cases'; 'a 10 per cent rise in self-harm referrals'; 'therapy that reduces substance misuse problems') but not for the individual case.

Using these 'headings' or 'categories' rather than just *saying what happened* carries several risks.

You can't make a detailed assessment of risk

Knowing that someone 'has substance misuse issues' tells you nothing. Does it mean they smoke cigarettes and a joint of cannabis once a week? Does it mean they're an intravenous heroin user spending £300 a week? Say what's happening. For example, 'there are issues of substance misuse and physical chastisement in the home, leading to Amy self-harming' could mean:

1. 'Mum drank a litre of vodka (which she does at least four times a week) and hit Amy with a metal stick. As a result, Amy jumped off a bridge intending to kill herself,' or

2. 'Mum smoked a joint of cannabis, argued with Amy and slapped her. Afterwards, Amy made superficial cuts to her wrists.'

Neither situation is good, but 1 is decidedly more serious than 2. Using general terms for a specific incident misses the detail, and the detail helps you assess needs and risk.

The Signs of Safety Model (Turnell and Edwards 1999) uses 'danger statements' to make this point. Rather than 'we are concerned about...', Signs of Safety encourages practitioners to talk in terms of 'we are afraid that ... could happen'. Rather than saying 'we are concerned about Ms Smith's substance use' consider 'we are worried that Ms Smith will take another overdose and be hospitalised or even die as a result, leaving her children bereaved and with no one to care for them'.

You sanitise the issue

I return again to Stephen King's concept of 'writing as telepathy'. If you tell a judge there was a 'physical abuse incident', this fails to plant a real picture of events in the judge's mind. Telling a judge 'Mr Smith pushed a cloth down Ms Jones' throat while telling her "you're dead now you bitch", then head-butted her' has far more effect.

You may find it tempting to 'sanitise' your writing when talking about sexual offences in particular. I've seen the following terms used interchangeably and often confused:

- rape

- sexual abuse

- sexual exploitation

- underage sex

- sexually inappropriate behaviour

- sexualised behaviour

- sexual experimentation

- having sex.

If in doubt, just *say what happened!* But this can be hard: you might find yourself having to write disturbing facts in explicit detail. It's reasonable not to keep repeating the same details over and over, but you can't exclude the details from your reports altogether. I've read many reports about sexual abuse where I've been unable to find out what actually happened beyond 'a sexual incident'.

Example 1

I read a 45-page assessment about a 14-year-old girl, which used the term 'sexually inappropriate behaviour' 29 times. There was no mention of what this behaviour was. I asked the author, who said he didn't know. I went back to the referrer (a head teacher) who also didn't know. Only when I spoke to the class teacher who first used the phrase could they tell me, 'she flirts with boys in class, in a really awkward way, so she makes herself look foolish'. Surely, awkward and unsuccessful flirting with peers aged 14 is nearly universal. This example demonstrates the dangers that, by using 'headings', you can form a skewed idea of risk, and lose the facts that lie behind your analysis.

Example 2

At the other end of the scale, I've had to challenge professionals for using the term 'sexualised behaviour' to refer to a 12-year-old girl having sex for money at the request of her 19-year-old boyfriend. The terms 'rape', 'sexual abuse' and 'sexual exploitation' are more applicable here, but it's even more helpful to just say what happened.

See **Taking it further** for some useful definitions of key terms. Bear in mind that 'sexually inappropriate' depends on a notion of what *would* be appropriate. The term 'child prostitution' is arguably a contradiction in terms and implies consent where none can be given (Rodriguez 2011), so I recommend avoiding this term altogether.

You may end up addressing a specific issue with a generic response

It's tempting to try to 'categorise' human beings and the complexities of their lives, and part of the managerialisation of social work involves trying to assign a service to a need based on a 'heading'. For example: 'this person has a substance misuse issue, so we'll refer them to the substance misuse team'; 'this person has been involved in domestic violence, so we'll refer them to the domestic violence service'; 'this person shows inappropriate behaviour, we'll refer them to counselling for behaviour management'.

This approach risks losing the nuances and causes relevant to an individual situation. Your approach to a couple who shout at each other every night should be different to your approach to a mother whose partner has threatened to kill her and branded her with hot metal, even though both cases involved 'domestic incidents'. A teenager who smokes cannabis with his friends at the weekends has different needs to a teenager who steals in order to buy crack cocaine every day.

People defy easy categorisation, and using generic terms can obscure (and therefore perpetuate) complex problems.

THE DANGERS OF JARGON

'Jargon' overlaps with the 'headings' discussed above, but also includes management-speak and needlessly long or obscure words to get a point across.

Hopkins (1998) said: 'social services departments are flooded with macho-drenched business-speak. And sadly rather than washing their hands of it, managers are taking to the waters.' This trend seems to have continued, although social workers are far from the only professionals guilty of this – Healy (2012) notes that doctors and engineers aren't expected to write in plain English, but social workers are.

The use of spoken and written jargon resembles Frankfurt's (2005) definition of 'bullshit': a 'deliberate misrepresentation *short* of lying' usually designed to cast the speaker/writer in a particular light. In *On Bullshit* (despite the title, a serious and concise philosophical essay), Frankfurt warns that using bullshit even makes it harder to tell the truth, more so than using lies: while lying has a negative 'truth value' and telling the truth has a positive truth value, bullshit has no truth value. For example:

> **I have come to the conclusion as a result of my assessment that in the view of the local authority there are serious concerns about the issues in the family. The parents have not engaged with services and are inappropriate in their substandard care of the children, causing physical neglect and emotional harm and having a deleterious effect on the children's welfare while failing to meet their needs. Looking forward we need to imbue their parental capacity with an increased proactivity under the auspices of a SMART intervention under a child in need which the parents should consistently engage with.**

This passage is 100 words long and manages to say absolutely nothing. It does, however, give two impressions:

1. I have identified myself as a professional who writes like a professional.
2. I don't like what these parents are doing.

Saying to the parents 'you need to clean the cat poo off the floor and let the family support worker in when she knocks' communicates much more than the passage above.

There are two immediate problems with this kind of jargon:

1. The service user doesn't know what you're talking about.
2. *You* don't know what you're talking about.

The second point is demonstrated every time a professional can't explain what they mean when asked for an example.

This advice meets surprising hostility in the workplace. Social workers and managers frequently tell me 'but we have to use long words to sound more professional'. No you don't, and this isn't just my view: Judge Lea criticised a social worker for writing a report that 'might as well be in a foreign language' and said that using long words to make simple points cast significant doubt on whether a social worker could properly communicate with a service user (Silman 2015). Judge Lea included examples from the report in his ruling:

> **I do not intend to address the couple's relationship suffice it to say it is imbued with ambivalence: both having many commonalities emanating from their histories that create what could be a long lasting connection or alternative relationship that are a reflection of this. Such is this connection they may collude to undermine the placement.**

And when the social worker wrote, 'I asked her to convey a narrative about her observations in respect of [the mother and father's] relationship', Judge Lea asked: 'What would be wrong in saying "I asked her to tell me"?'

Ofsted (2015) also found that:

> **Language that social workers use in written assessments and resulting plans [is] often unclear and uses jargon. This made it difficult for families to fully understand decisions and judgements and what needed to change to make things better for children.**

> **Professional jargon ... minimises the concerns and severity of some situations. For example ... 'three previous instances of domestic abuse' could range from a verbal altercation to a serious physical assault. If the worker had explicitly described [it] ... this would have more impact. Minimising concerns ... can make it difficult for children and families to understand the assessment decisions and progress any plans and actions.**

> **The language used in written assessment and planning documents was often unclear, over-complicated, detracted from the concerns raised and was unhelpful to families.**

> **Workers tried to 'over-professionalise' their written work and consequently did not communicate their thoughts and findings well.**

Always read back to yourself what you've written: if it feels unnatural to say, it probably feels unnatural to read.

Think of your vocabulary like the referee in a football match – if they do their job well, no one will notice them.

Professionals often use unnecessarily long words because they feel insecure about their professionalism. They think that because some well-respected experts use complicated words, they can show the same expertise by using the same vocabulary. This is like trying to run as fast as an Olympic sprinter by buying the same trainers: the vocabulary doesn't make you more skilful, your skills do.

Use their own words

Another sad consequence of jargon is that you miss the opportunity to use people's own words – 'primary evidence'. Consider these two paragraphs, describing the same situation:

> **The child disclosed that they were experiencing mental and physical harm due to the incidents and concerns involving their parents, including domestic violence and substance misuse.**

and

> **Ryan said: 'When mum and dad hit each other I take my sisters upstairs, then I tell them to stop fighting. Dad calls me a fucking baby and one time he punched me. I slapped him back. Him and mum get sleepy when they've had too much drugs. That's when I burn myself with their lighter, when everyone's asleep so they can't see.'**

The second is far more powerful – again, remember the people reading your report may not have met the family and have not seen and heard what you have. If you leave out the evidence of your own eyes and ears, you're leaving out much of what makes you the expert on this family.

It's also more useful. Confronting parents (or a judge) with the children's own words can be much more effective than telling them what a group of professionals think. While no assessment can ever be entirely 'objective' (and we should not pretend it can), using direct quotes is more transparent.

Say what you mean

Social workers want to support people. But the word 'support' is meaningless on its own. A conclusion that 'the family should be offered support' is really saying 'I care, and someone should probably do something, but I'm not going to say who, what or how'. It sounds 'professional' but communicates, and achieves, nothing.

Example

I chaired a tense meeting where both the head teacher and the child's parents were saying 'they need support', angry that 'support' hadn't been provided. I asked each of them outside the meeting room, alone, what they meant by 'support'. The parents said 'we need to move to a bigger house, we need childcare, and we need help with money'.

The head teacher said, 'really I don't think the child is safe at home and probably needs a foster placement'.

The same applies to:

- concerns

- issues

- dysfunctions

- problems

- help

- services

- a support package

- therapy (unspecified)

- work with the family/a piece of work

- and others.

If you think there's a problem, say what it is. If you think you need to do something (or someone else needs to) then say who and what. If you don't know, ask your managers and colleagues for ideas. I suspect that the use of vague terms often masks the fact that the social worker doesn't know what to do. If the specific work is outside your expertise (e.g., what kind of therapy to provide), work out whose advice you need and find out how to get it.

LANGUAGE AS A TOOL OF OPPRESSION

I could never do justice to the extensive literature on the oppressive power of language. See **Taking it further** for references to some of those who can.

However, any discussion of writing in social work must include the power dynamics involved in our choice of words, which reveal 'the ideologies that underpin our views of the world and the power relations inherent within those' (Dominelli 2002a).

Despite language being a 'vehicle' for the principles of anti-oppressive and anti-discriminatory practice (Turney 2014), it is often ignored (Marcoccio 1995).

'Language is embedded within power relations which are often implicit in its usage' (Dominelli 2002b), and the most dangerous part of oppression through language is when you don't know you're doing it.

The previous discussion on jargon and other common writing problems is not just about professionalism and communication, but about how you interact with service users.

Damaging assumptions

Using overt or derogatory discrimination in language is usually challenged, although some terms persist. I've heard social workers use 'submissive' to describe a South Asian woman, 'angry' to describe a black service user, or 'Zionist' as a synonym for Jewish, betraying underlying attitudes and assumptions.

The assumption of 'the default' is much more dangerous since it carries an implicit assumption of 'us and them', of 'normal versus abnormal'.

I have worked in a local authority where all service users were recorded as being 'Christian: Church of England' unless they stated otherwise. The rationale given was that 'this is the default religion'. Even though the use of 'straight' to mean heterosexual is widely acceptable (indeed, it originated among homosexual men in the early twentieth century – Henry 1941), its use suggests cisgender heterosexuality as 'normal' and other sexualities as somehow 'crooked' or 'bent'.

The same theme applies when a characteristic is highlighted despite bearing no relationship to the problem: for example the media sometimes focus on a suspect being Muslim, when the offence has nothing to do with religion, while suspects are rarely described as 'Christian' (Allegretti 2015). In social work practice, I have frequently heard someone's minority religion, sexuality, gender identity or disability discussed in depth regardless of relevance to the specific issues involved. While all aspects of people's identity should be properly recognised, treating someone's identity as central to their involvement in abuse or neglect is usually unhelpful, and serves only to emphasise the person's 'difference' in an arbitrary way.

Two words to avoid

Many words discriminate or oppress, but the following two are particularly subtle and insidious:

'Inappropriate'

This word is subjective, depending on your assumptions about 'appropriate' behaviour. A head teacher reported 'inappropriate sexual behaviour' to me: a six-year-old boy kissing another boy. While I could not prove it, I doubted that she would have used the same term to describe a boy and a girl kissing. Another teacher made a referral for a child whose parents were known 'swingers' due to their concern that the parents' 'inappropriate lifestyle' would inherently put the child at risk.

Munby (2014) ruled that Social Services are not 'guardians of morality' and had no business trying to separate a child from a father who was a member of the English Defence League and had a prior conviction for sex with a 13-year-old when he was 17. The courts take a dim view of social workers criticising families' lifestyles, decisions or personalities, *unless* they are causing significant harm.

However, social workers have a duty to intervene when someone's behaviour is damaging another person, and to intervene regardless of the person's identity. Social workers can also fail to protect when they make too much allowance for someone's 'difference'. But even where it is right to challenge someone's behaviour, the word 'inappropriate' won't help you make a case. Say what the behaviour is, and what effects it has.

'Aggressive'

Again, social workers encounter people who pose a genuine risk of physical violence, and who can put others in fear for their safety. You should never ignore these risks. However, the term 'aggressive' doesn't help you keep someone safe.

The courts say social workers cannot use a parent's 'aggression' as a reason to escalate their involvement. In a judicial review (Ministry of Justice 2013), the court found that a local authority acted unlawfully when they escalated a referral to a child protection investigation on the basis that the parents became angry and threatened to make a complaint when confronted with an anonymous allegation.

The problem is that, like the 'headings' discussed previously, 'aggression' can mean too many different things to be useful. It could mean a service user being angry that they have been kept waiting for an appointment, or it could mean someone making a threat to kill. I have seen the word used to overstate and understate the risk involved.

Example 1

A teacher said a child was not safe with his mother, due to her 'aggression'. They linked the mother's 'aggression' to a risk of physical violence to the child (although no violence had ever been alleged). I challenged the teacher to say what the mother had said. Initially she would only say 'she became aggressive and threatened me'. Eventually she said the mother told her 'I'm going to make a complaint and sue you' and this made her intimidated.

Example 2

A social work report referred more than ten times to 'aggression between the parents'. It never gave details. Only by reading the original police reports did I find that the father had strangled the mother until she nearly lost consciousness, had held a knife to her throat and said he would kill her.

The use of the same word in both contexts (and many in-between) makes the term unhelpful without detail.

More sinister is the overlap between vagueness and unconscious bias. Phelps and Thomas (2003) found that, in an MRI scanner, white subjects showed a heightened 'fear response' in the amygdala when shown black faces compared to when they were shown white faces. Black subjects similarly showed a fear response to white faces, although to a reduced extent. Using words that reflect how you *felt* about someone's behaviour is more likely to reflect bias than words that reflect what the person said and did.

PROJECT IMPLICIT

See **Take it further** for the link to Project Implicit, run since 1998 to test unconscious biases regarding gender, ethnicity, sexuality, disability and age. You may be surprised by your results: the majority of people taking the test, even those identifying consciously as liberal, tolerant and egalitarian, displayed inherent biases against other groups.

Vague terminology allows more unconscious prejudice to slip through the net.

CHAPTER SUMMARY

Aims

Your writing has power and significance. Your professional values, your professional skills and the service user's experience and needs should come through more than the language of the process involved.

Your writing should:

- Tell a story.

- Be readable by anyone.

- Make the reader better-informed, by transmitting your understanding from your head into theirs.

Your reports should:

- Be accountable. Use 'I' where it makes sense to do so.

- Be balanced.

- Use different structures depending on the situation.

- User service users' own words.

Avoid:

- **The passive voice.** 'Mr Smith told me that Mr Jones hit Eddie' is far more useful than 'it has been reported that Eddie has been hit'.

- **Headings.** 'Domestic violence' is a useful term for several incidents; 'Mr Jones punched Mrs Jones in the face and spat in her eye' is both more accurate and powerful for an individual case.

- **Jargon.** If you wouldn't use it in (polite) spoken conversation, don't write it.

- **Subjective terms**, especially adjectives such as 'aggressive' and 'inappropriate'. If something is worrying, describe it as it is, rather than adding an unnecessary and unhelpful layer of interpretation.

 TAKING IT FURTHER

Ferguson, I and Woodward, R (2009) *Radical Social Work in Practice: Making a Difference*, University of Chicago Press

Hopkins, G (1998) *Plain English for Social Services*, Russell House Publishing

King, S (2000) *On Writing: A Memoir of the Craft*, Charles Scribner's Sons

Project Implicit, https://implicit.harvard.edu/implicit/takeatest.html

On discourse, language and oppression

Bosmajian, H (1983) *The Language of Oppression*, University Press of America

Dominelli, L (2002a) *Anti-Oppressive Social Work Theory and Practice*, Palgrave Macmillan

Dominelli, L (2002b) *Feminist Social Work Theory and Practice*, Palgrave Macmillan

Foucault, M (1969) *The Archaeology of Knowledge*, Pantheon

Foucault, M (1970) *The Order of Things*, Pantheon

Marcoccio, K (1995) Identifying oppression in language: the power of words, *Canadian Social Work Review/Revue Canadienne De Service Social*, 12(2)

Turney, D (2014) Deconstructing the language of anti-oppressive practice in social work, in C Cocker and T Hafford-Letchfield (eds.), *Re-Thinking Anti-Discriminatory and Anti-Oppressive Theories for Social Work Practice*, Palgrave Macmillan, pp. 168–182

Definitions of key terms linked to sexual abuse

Legal terms, www.cps.gov.uk/legal/p_to_r/rape_and_sexual_offences/soa_2003_and_soa_1956/#a03

Sexual exploitation, www.nspcc.org.uk/preventing-abuse/child-abuse-and-neglect/child-sexual-exploitation/what-is-child-sexual-exploitation/

Sexual abuse, www.workingtogetheronline.co.uk/glossary/sex_abuse.html

Healthy sexual behaviour in children (as a yardstick for what *inappropriate* or sexualised behaviour might be), www.nspcc.org.uk/preventing-abuse/keeping-children-safe/healthy-sexual-behaviour-children-young-people/

REFERENCES

Aas, K (2004) From narrative to database: technological change and penal culture, *Punishment & Society*, 6(4), 379–393

Allegretti, A (2015) *Mail on Sunday* apologies for offensive 'Muslim gang's attack on immigration van' story, *Huffington Post*, 30 July

Calhoun, C (1995) *Critical Social Theory: Culture, History and the Challenge of Difference*, Blackwell

Dominelli, L (2002a) *Anti-Oppressive Social Work Theory and Practice*, Palgrave Macmillan

Dominelli, L (2002b) *Feminist Social Work Theory and Practice*, Palgrave Macmillan

Featherstone, B and Peckover, S (2007) Letting them get away with it: fathers, domestic violence and child welfare, *Critical Social Policy*, 27(2), 181–202

Ferguson, I and Woodward, R (2009) *Radical Social Work in Practice: Making a Difference*, University of Chicago Press

Forbes, F, Duffy, J C., Mok, J and Lemvig, J (2003) Early intervention service for non-abusing parents of victims of child sexual abuse, *The British Journal of Psychiatry*, 183(1), 66–72.

Frankfurt, H (2005) *On Bullshit*, Princeton University Press

Healy, K (2012) *Writing Skills for Social Workers*, Sage

Henry, G (1941) *Sex Variants: A Study of Homosexual Patterns*, Hoeber

Hopkins, G (1998) *Plain English for Social Services*, Russell House Publishing

Katz, J (2003) *Building a Big Tent Approach to Ending Men's Violence. Building Partners Initiative*, United States Department of Justice, see also TED Talk, www.ted.com/talks/jackson_katz_violence_against_women_it_s_a_men_s_issue?language=en

King, S (2000) *On Writing: A Memoir of the Craft*, Charles Scribner's Sons

Marcoccio, K (1995) Identifying impression in language: the power of words, *Canadian Social Work Review/Revue Canadienne De Service Social*, 12(2), 146–158

Ministry of Justice (2013) *Judicial Review: R(AB and CD) v Haringey London Borough Council [2013] EWHC 416 (Admin)*, Ministry of Justice

Munby J (2014) Judgement on Re. A [2015] EWFC 11

Nunnally, M and Bitan, Y (2006) Time to get off this pig's back? The human factors aspects of the mismatch between device and real-world knowledge in the health care environment, *Journal of Patient Safety*, 2(3), 124–131

Ofsted (2015) *Children in Need and Child Protection: Quality of Early Help and Social Work Assessments*, Ofsted *(full disclosure: I was a contributor to this report, although I did not write the conclusions quoted here)*

Phelps, E and Thomas, L (2003) Race, behavior and the brain: the role of neuroimaging in understanding complex social behaviors, *Political Psychology*, 24(4), 747–758

Rasmussen, T (2000) *Social Theory and Communication Technology*, Ashgate

Rodriguez, J (2011) *Slavery in the Modern World: A History of Political, Social, and Economic Oppression*, 2 vols., ABC-CLIO

Silman, J (2015) Social worker criticised by judge for using jargon in court report, *Community Care*, 15 August

Stevenson, L (2014) Judge criticises social workers for 'grossly overstated' adoption evidence, *Community Care*, 28 November

Turnell, A and Edwards, S (1999) *Signs of Safety: A Solution and Safety Oriented Approach to Child Protection Casework*, W.W. Norton & Company

Turney, D (2014) Deconstructing the language of anti-oppressive practice in social work, in C. Cocker and T. Hafford-Letchfield (eds.), *Re-Thinking Anti-Discriminatory and Anti-Oppressive Theories for Social Work Practice*, Palgrave Macmillan, pp. 168–182

Analysis

'We make our world significant by the courage of our questions and the depth of our answers.'

Carl Sagan (1980)

WHAT THIS CHAPTER COVERS

- Trying to unpick the truth.

- What to include: the Information Pyramid.

- How to analyse rather than just describe.

- How to sharpen your analysis.

- Introduction to anti-oppressive issues in your analysis.

- The link between analysis and plans.

- Example of a table used to check consistency between accounts.

TRUTH OR FICTION?

The riddle of the three ants:

There are three ants walking in a straight line on the ground. There are no shadows, no reflective surfaces and the ants are of sound mind. There are no other ants in sight.

The first ant says 'there are no ants in front of me, and there are two ants behind me'.

The second ant says 'there is one ant in front of me, and there is one ant behind me'.

The third ant says 'there are two ants in front of me, and there is an ant behind me'.

How is this possible?

The answer is later in this section. Tip: in three years of using this riddle in lectures, only one social worker has ever got the answer right. By contrast, when I asked one high-school child they got it right immediately.

A WORD OF CAUTION: FINDINGS IN COURT

This section is about trying to find out the truth.

You may find yourself writing a report for court where you are required 'not to give a view as to the facts', since this would amount to you pre-empting a 'finding of fact' by a judge.

However, this doesn't mean you assess as though none of the facts are established – you have to make at least some assumptions about what has happened.

You may find it useful to:

*   Qualify some statements with words to the effect of 'based on the information in the chronology/bundle/witness statements/etc.'.

*   Provide 'parallel analysis', within reason, where there is a dispute about a key fact. For example, if you're assessing the risk posed by a mother accused of injuring her child, your analysis will be different depending on whether she did in fact injure her child. You might produce two analyses: one in the event that the court finds she did not (this may be a short analysis) and one in the event that the court finds she did.

*   Make it clear when you've taken an assumption about a fact.

*   Provide 'best case' and 'worst case' analyses. Sometimes, you might find that even taking every possible negative assumption about the disputed facts about someone (e.g., a prospective carer), you still assess them as suitable. At other times, you might find that even taking every possible positive assumption about the facts, you would still find the person unsuitable. Such an analysis can 'cover' a range of underlying facts that you are currently uncertain about.

While you should always treat people with an open mind, the unfortunate reality is that in social work, particularly in safeguarding, people will sometimes lie to you. Service users, carers and professionals can all shape or invent facts.

You can help maintain an open mind by focusing on your use of language. The word 'said' is sadly underused in social work. Professionals persist in using the following alternatives:

- stated

- confessed

- was very open about

- was of the opinion that

- disclosed

- argued that

- noted

- reported

- admitted

- cited

- informed

- pointed out

- claimed

- was clear that

- was adamant that

- was able to express their view that

- articulated that

- verbalised

- vocalised

- insisted

- declared

- expressed

- held their hands up about

- iterated forcefully that

- revealed

- … and many more.

This isn't just me being pedantic: most of the above contain a different connotation from 'said' – many suggest that the writer believes or is sceptical about the speaker. Saying 'Mr Brown was very open about smoking three joints of cannabis earlier that day' or 'Ms Campbell confessed that she had been impatient with her mother and shouted at her' isn't just saying what they said: it suggests that you believe them.

This can be dangerous, considering a common strategy of effective liars is to 'own up' to something moderate to give them more credibility when they deny something more serious. Mr Brown, above, might have smoked crack cocaine as well. Ms Campbell might have beaten her mother. In both cases, admitting to something less serious may convince a professional that they are honest.

The answer to the riddle is that the third ant is *lying*. In lectures, nearly all social workers and students missed this, even though the riddle includes all the relevant facts, and a direct contradiction of those facts by the third ant.

In isolation, it is near-impossible to have a conversation with someone and know whether they are telling the truth, unless they contradict themselves within the same conversation. Even polygraphs (Lykken 1998) and voice-stress analysis (Eriksson and Lacerda 2007) are inaccurate despite their enduring reputations – both are, like an empathic human listener, effective at detecting *stress*, but it is too much of a leap to assume that stress necessarily indicates lying (or that being relaxed indicates truthfulness).

Using 'said' is simple, easy and avoids baseless suggestions of truthfulness or deception. Using it repeatedly will not make your report 'less professional' but it may make it less credulous. When someone says something to you, all you really know is that they have said it.

Too many social work assessments treat the interviewee's responses as the facts. Usually people tell you the truth. But always 'triangulate' their words against other information. What do other members of the household and wider family say? What do professionals say? What does the interviewee say, at different points in time (evidenced in the old files)? Is what they are saying plausible?

This can be uncomfortable. Should you write in your report that someone is a liar? Should you accuse them of lying to their face? What if they turn out to be telling the truth, and your credibility is ruined?

Indeed, you can never be certain that someone is definitely lying, or definitely telling the truth. You might be proved wrong either way. But the courts don't require certainty: the Family Court and Court of Protection both require that you make a case on a balance of probabilities.

It is reasonable to describe someone's account as 'inconsistent' or 'consistent' with other evidence.

In some cases, you might find it useful to create a table, laying out what each source tells you about different points of fact. It may help to include words along the lines of 'this does not pre-empt a finding of fact in court, but is designed to help focus my analysis'.

I have included an example of how such a table might fit into a report at the end of this chapter.

Convincing a court of someone's dishonesty is not the end of the argument. While the judge will take a dim view of the person's lie, they are still principally concerned with a just outcome. People lie to the authorities for many reasons, some rational and some not. Proving that a parent is lying about something of personal importance to them, but that does not affect the safety of a child, does not affect your case. Proving that a parent is lying about their heroin use when this is a key reason for them being unable to provide care, on the other hand, is more significant.

Use your imagination

In Chapter 2, I used the Availability Heuristic (Tversky and Kahneman 1973) and the Picture Superiority Effect (Nelson et al. 1976) to argue for absorbing 'dry', written information *before* doing a visit, since you may be more influenced by the more vivid, visual sensations of meeting someone face-to-face.

In other words, when you go into a nice, clean home and speak to some polite, articulate people, this can give you a false sense of security. Social work requires empathy: not only in wishing someone well, but also in imagining the reality of their world. You need to look past the presenting image and form a mental picture of what has happened between these people.

Example

You are working for a child protection team, and have removed a baby at birth from their parents, who are both heroin addicts and regularly fight each other. The parents met in their mid-teens when both were in care, and they have been addicted to drugs and alcohol ever since. The paternal grandmother contacts you and says she can care for her grandchild. Unlike the parents, who are both very angry and unpredictable (the father has hit a contact supervisor and the mother has threatened to stab a social worker), the grandmother is calm, polite and seems very sensible. You are asked to assess her suitability as a carer, although both parents object. You visit her at her home, which is beautiful, and feel very positive about her as a long-term carer.

In this example, it is possible to overlook the following questions:

• Why was the father in care?

• Is there anything in the father's childhood that has contributed to his dangerous and dysfunctional lifestyle?

• Why are the parents objecting to her as a carer (given that the alternative may be for their baby to be adopted)?

The answers to all of these may show the grandmother to be blameless. Perhaps she was in a violent relationship that has ended, and she is now trying to repair the damage this caused. Perhaps the father inherits (and has learned) traits from a violent, drug-addicted grandfather, rather than from the grandmother. And perhaps the parents object to her having custody of their child because she criticises them about their lifestyle and has tried to 'interfere' to get them to give up drugs. This might bode well for the grandmother to care for the children.

However, the picture may be less rosy. Perhaps the father was in care because of a chaotic, emotionally abusive environment at home. Perhaps he began using drugs as an escape from a miserable home life and alcoholic parents. And perhaps the parents object because they fear the grandmother will subject their child to the same experience as she put the father through, knowing that she has now become more articulate and able to manipulate people. This would be far more concerning.

Whenever assessing a grandparent to care for a child, or whenever assessing a parent to care for a vulnerable adult, always start with a picture of how that person raised their own children. This is not necessarily the whole story: someone who was a poor parent may have learned from their mistakes and moved on, but you would have to evidence this change.

I once read in an assessment: 'The police reports said that Mr Smith was very violent with a long history of assaults, but he was not at all violent when I met him.' You will often not see the most significant issues play out during a visit. A neglected home or a pronounced mental illness will probably be much more 'visible' than a pattern of sexual abuse, high-functioning addiction or domestic violence.

A false choice: not just 'true or malicious'

In an investigation, social workers often ask 'is this allegation true, or is it malicious?' It may be neither.

Instead of an either/or choice, where a claim is either true and made in good faith, or false and made maliciously, consider the following table:

	Good faith	**Bad faith**
Correct	True	'Gloating' (epicaricacy or *schadenfreude*: pleasure from the discomfort of others)
Incorrect	Mistaken	Malicious

Example 1: A neighbour hears a child scream followed by an adult shouting at them. They call the police. The investigation finds the child was being hit with objects by their parents. The allegation was correct, and made in good faith.

Example 2: An aunt sees their nephew covered in bruises, just after the mother said that she was having problems with her new boyfriend who she says is 'a bit rough'. The aunt calls Social Services. It turns out that the child fell off playground equipment at school that day causing bruises, and is very happy at home. The aunt was incorrect, but acted in good faith: not 'malicious' but mistaken.

Example 3: A father calls Social Services anonymously to say that his ex-wife is beating her children and taking lots of drugs. An investigation finds that her children are happy, there are no signs of abuse and the wife is a lifelong teetotaller, who has just gone to court to require her ex-husband to pay child support. The allegation seems to be both incorrect and in bad faith (malicious).

Example 4: A grandmother calls Social Services to report her daughter and son-in-law for being drunk in charge of their children on a regular basis. She knows this because she used to get drunk with them every day in front of the children, but they evicted her after a fight and they've been drinking the alcohol she bought. While the allegation was spiteful, it was still true. However, you should bear the grandmother's bad faith in mind when considering other information she provides.

WHAT TO INCLUDE

One of the aims of the New Public Outline for child care proceedings was to reduce the amount of paperwork submitted to the court (Munby 2013). Social work assessments in children's and adults' services tend to be overlong (addressed in this section) and overly descriptive (see next section).

Again, the issue is often not skill, but fear. Even if you know the important issues in a case, you can still become defensive when writing a report, especially for court. You know in principle that your report should be concise, but then what if you leave out something important? Under pressure, social workers often resort to writing everything they know, and everything in their records, into an assessment.

This is another false choice: you don't have to choose between being thorough and being succinct. The mistake is to treat every document as though it's the only document anyone is every going to read.

The Information Pyramid

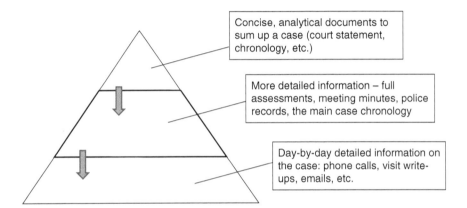

Imagine that the first level of the pyramid – the application to the court – consists of 20 pages of statement, chronology and care plan.

The second level contains 100 pages: every assessment produced in the last two years, a longer chronology and some police records and minutes of conferences.

The third level, in principle, would run to hundreds or even thousands of pages: every note of every visit and conversation on the case, every email sent, old files going back several years and financial records of spending by your department.

The judge and the other parties read your 20 pages. Some of it is not disputed. However, the lawyer for the father complains that it is untrue that their client is a 'dangerous and violent man' as you have said in your statement.

So the judge dips down a level, into the second level, and finds the parenting assessment carried out on the father (*not* every single document from the second layer). The judge reads the 15-page assessment, which concludes the father is violent based on his history of assaulting his wife, ex-wife and stepchildren.

But the lawyer says this is untrue, and that the social workers have twisted the evidence. Your assessment refers to police records, and to a conversation with the father where he admitted hitting his stepchildren. The father says the records are wrong and he never said that.

So the judge dips down another level, and requests the relevant case notes and the police records: a total of another ten pages (*not* every case note ever written). The case note was written up immediately after a meeting with the father and other professionals, where he said he had hit his stepchildren. The police records include only one conviction for assault, but several arrests where the victim has withdrawn their statement.

So in this example, the judge has read only 45 pages, not several hundred. The key is not to put every case note into the statements and assessments, but to make sure that the statement refers to assessments where relevant, and the assessments refer to primary evidence.

Include the positive

Your report should be balanced, recognising the positives in a person's life as well as the negatives. It's a mistake to think your report – even a statement for court – has to be a relentless and unequivocal condemnation of a parent or carer. Failing to recognise what is going well does not make you look consistent and firm, it makes you look biased. People rarely have a life with nothing but dysfunction, and even the most dangerous homes can have some happy times. Acknowledging these doesn't weaken your case, it strengthens it by showing you've been open-minded and fair.

Avoid diversions

Some things are easier to talk about than others. Analysing whether someone is telling you the truth is hard. Working out attendance at meetings is easy. Predicting whether a child will be unhappy at home is hard. Listing their attendance at school and medical appointments is easy.

No wonder, then, that many assessments and plans focus on the indisputable, objective facts of immunisations, school attendance or whether someone has attended a course. These are not unimportant, but can be a diversion from the real issue. Someone can still be at risk if their carer has attended every meeting and taken them to every daycare session. Similarly, someone can be chaotic and often miss appointments, but still provide a safe and caring home.

ANALYSIS VERSUS DESCRIPTION
Causation, information and implication

I read 300 assessments for a research project (unpublished), and found that while they all contained a factual account of a problem, only half contained an analysis of what this meant for the children, while only a quarter contained any exploration of what was causing the problem.

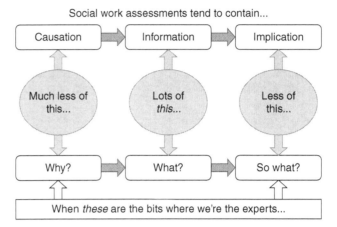

Social work assessments tend to contain...

This observation was consistent with what Brandon et al. (2008) found: assessments were too 'descriptive' and not sufficiently 'dynamic':

> **Too often, the Assessment Framework appears to be used in a flat, non-dynamic way. This leads to the accumulation of facts but little appreciation of how to formulate the facts in the manner of a clear explanation.**

My model above breaks down analysis into the 'causation' and 'implication' stages of a 'causation-information-implication' analysis (better described as a 'why-what-so what?' model).

Example

The mother drinks very heavily (*information*). She drinks because she feels depressed and isolated, and unhappy in her relationship (*causation*). This affects her baby as she is often unable to respond to his demands, and it affects her teenage daughter as she is teased for her mum being the 'local drunk', making her unhappy (*implication* – note how it differs for different children).

Many assessments only focus on the mother's drinking as a 'concern' without linking it to the impact on the children (which would justify professional intervention) or the causes of her drinking (which would inform any plans to help her).

Chapman (2004) finds in his work on systems theory that:

> **the ability to grasp a bigger picture or a different perspective is not usually constrained by lack of information. The critical constraints are usually in the way that the individual thinks and the assumptions that they make – both of which are usually unknown to that individual.**

In other words, while it is important to gather and present information, the effectiveness of your assessment is based on your analysis of the information, *and* in your own self-awareness of how you analyse (see **Analysis as a means of oppression or empowerment**, below).

Using analytical and theoretical models

During your social work degree (and hopefully afterwards) you will have learned theories and techniques to analyse the complexities of someone's life. I couldn't do justice to whole fields of study in one chapter, so I encourage you to explore models of analysis including:

- Prochaska et al.'s (1994) Stages of Change model. Your analysis of someone trying to overcome a problem (e.g., an addiction) might place them at some point along Prochaska's model of Pre-Contemplation, Contemplation, Determination, Action, Relapse and Maintenance.

- Berne (1964)'s 'games' and Transactional Analysis. You may find that the interactions between two people in a household resemble 'parent to child' strokes, even when both (or neither) are adults, or you may find 'crossed transactions', for example where a 'child to parent' stroke is countered with a 'child to child' or 'adult to adult' interaction – addressing these interactions may be key to improving relationships within the home.

- Turnell and Edwards' (1999) Signs of Safety model (also see Parton and O'Byrne 2000): you may use this model in order to build meaningful working relationships with a family where there is danger to a child, exploring both danger and safety factors and working out 'what are we worried about?', 'what is working well?' and 'what needs to change?' as a constructive way to solve problems using a family's resources.

- Conflict theory approaches challenging entrenched power systems, highlighting where a power imbalance is so great the struggle becomes invisible. Freire (1970) argues that the radical 'does not believe that they own the historical process or that they are the suppressed's liberator, no, they are involved in the historical process to fight by their side'. Dominelli (2002) likewise recommends valuing, rather than simply noting, the words and views of service users, and redefining your professional role so as not to add further layers of oppression.

- Attachment theories, created by Bowlby (1969) and developed by Ainsworth et al. (1978). You may use Ainsworth's categories of attachment in your analysis, and draw inferences about possible future relationship patterns. Crittenden and Landini (2011)'s Dynamic Maturational Model provides another version for analysis.

The use of theory and 'formal knowledge' (Munro 2004) causes anxiety for some social workers, who feel more comfortable using their 'gut feeling' about a case. Munro explores the difference between the intuitive and the analytical and shows why they do not conflict: an experienced social worker develops 'formal intuition': they still get a gut feeling when they read information or make an observation, but it is now an intuition based on experience and research.

Klein (1999) coins the term 'Recognition-Primed Decision-Making' (RPD) to describe what happens when a professional 'uses their experience' or 'trusts their gut': he identifies a complex series of mental steps that quickly build a picture of the likely cause of a problem and the likely outcome, using prior experience (the 'recognition' of key factors) and theoretical understanding. A less experienced worker uses a similar knowledge base but has less personal experience to draw on, and does so consciously rather than intuitively, to begin with.

QUOTING RESEARCH IN REPORTS

Social work assessments should be evidence-based, and the more comprehensive the assessment, the more research may be needed to justify the conclusions you reach.

However, many social workers feel anxiety about citing research. You may find the following rules of thumb helpful:

- Cite original research, not second-hand references. For example, it's acceptable to use Wikipedia or news articles to start researching a topic, but you'll need to read, and understand, the primary evidence.

- Only quote research that you've read and that you understand: imagine being asked (simple) questions about it, and make sure you'd be able to answer.

- Never refer vaguely to 'Research says...' – refer to a full reference at the bottom of the page or in a bibliography.

- Be honest. Acknowledge when the research is ambiguous or doesn't wholly support your position. Always search for neutral terms, for example, 'effects of cannabis on an unborn child' rather than 'cannabis damages unborn children' to get a representative sample on Google Scholar, LexisNexis, Research in Practice or a similar database.

- Use the research 'dynamically', i.e., incorporate it into your argument rather than letting it stand alone. For example, 'since Mr Scott has been teetotal for over a year, the research [citation] shows that his likelihood of relapsing over the next five years is less than 50 per cent. Therefore any consequences of his drinking are also less than 50 per cent likely to occur over the next few years.'

- Critically evaluate the research or the model. Don't treat any model as absolute and recognise how it makes approximations, not exact predictions: 'all models are wrong, but some are useful' (Box 1976).

Example:

Bad: 'Research tells us that sexual abuse has terrible effects on a child and they can suffer serious emotional harm (Smith 1985) so Mr Jones is a risk to his child.'

Good: 'Mr Jones says he would never abuse his child, even though he was convicted of raping an unrelated child of the same age. Research finds differing likelihoods of "cross-over" between abusing an unrelated and a related child: from 23 per cent[1] to 50 per cent[2] but these only count criminal convictions for sexual abuse, rather than findings on a balance of probability, so the true rate may be substantially higher. Whatever the true crossover rates, I consider this range an unacceptably high possibility that he will abuse his own daughter.'

[1] Abel, G (1988) Multiple paraphilic diagnoses among sex offenders, *Bulletin of the American Academy of Psychiatry and the Law*, 153, 166.

[2] Heil, P (2003) Crossover sexual offenses, *Sexual Abuse: A Journal of Research and Treatment*, 221, 232.

SHARPENING YOUR ANALYSIS

Make your argument 'flow'

Your assessment should not be a meaningless bureaucratic exercise to fulfil a statutory requirement. Your assessment should be a logical progression, from the evidence through the analysis to a conclusion and decision (or a recommendation to support a decision). It should help people (including the service user) make decisions and it should inform ongoing work.

A prescriptive framework can often interrupt the flow of your thinking: the more different boxes you have to jump between, the harder it is to maintain a coherent narrative. Segmented documents are fine for recording information, but less helpful for getting across a chain of thought – you will have to work harder to get a coherent narrative across.

Brown and Duguid (2000) differentiate information and knowledge in that 'knowledge requires a knower' and, while information lends itself to being picked up and moved around in discrete chunks, knowledge requires a wider understanding that is less easily broken up and put back together again. In your assessments you are trying to develop, and then communicate, *knowledge* rather than just information.

This is why your assessments will benefit from the habit of thorough, report-ready case notes: the 'information' sections of your report can be entered relatively quickly if you can add most of the words from your existing notes. This means you're not stuck typing in mundane details rather than concentrating on your analysis.

See Chapter 4 with regard to writing style.

Avoid 'mid-Atlantic thinking'

Imagine you're looking for someone. You know that they are either in London or New York. One place you would *not* search for them is the middle of the Atlantic ocean, even though this is the halfway point between the two.

Sometimes the seriousness of the situation can move up and down a 'sliding scale': a dirty home may get incrementally cleaner or dirtier day by day; a tense relationship may become more or less tolerable week by week. However, if a child says her stepfather has forced her to have sex with him, and he denies doing anything wrong, there is no 'middle ground'. An elderly man whose injury may have been caused by an ordinary fall or by being punched by his son either has or hasn't been abused.

This seems obvious, but can sometimes be fudged in an effort to achieve 'compromise' in a tense situation where the facts are unclear.

The risks of 'mid-Atlantic thinking' are:

- **Irrational analysis.** Social workers sometimes conclude a halfway version of events that makes little sense. They conclude that they can't prove a child's allegation, but that she may have believed she was raped. This doesn't make sense: either it happened (and she needs to be protected) or it didn't happen (and you need to make some sense of why she would have made a false allegation). Social workers may conclude that someone sustained an injury innocently but that 'better supervision' is required (even though safe, happy people sustain accidental injuries every day).

- **Ineffective plans.** Some safeguarding investigations conclude with the allegations 'unproven' but recommendations for a plan of monitoring or support work, even when no other problems have been identified. The reason is obvious: social workers cannot prove the allegation, but feel nervous that they could be wrong, so want to be seen to do something.

  If the concerns are unfounded and nothing happened, then the correct level of intervention afterwards is: absolutely nothing.

If someone is suffering abuse in their home, then 'monitoring' or low-key support work will have minimal protective effect. In fact, it could even reduce the level of safety, since social workers, schools, daycare and other professionals may feel a false sense of security thinking that 'something is being done' when nothing protective is happening.

Keep it simple. What's happened? Why has it happened? What's likely to happen in future? What are the implications of it happening? What should we do about it? The answers to these questions should flow together as one train of argument.

Categorising is *not* analysing

Platt and Turney (2013) argue against a 'technical-rational model' for making intervention decisions along a 'linear path of seriousness':

> **To reduce children's needs to a point on a measuring stick demonstrates a failure to understand the meaning and impact of the experience for that particular child ... the idea of a threshold as a single objectively defined point on a linear scale is unlikely to be feasible in the majority of cases.**

In other words, don't obsess over the question of 'does this case meet this criteria?' or 'does it meet the threshold for [service] or to hold [meeting]?'

The problems with the 'threshold-centred' approach are that:

- It encourages a tick-box or triage approach to analysing. Saying that someone meets the criteria for a 'child in need' or a 'child at risk' does not constitute an analysis. Putting someone in a broad category blurs the detail. Even people on a protection plan for abuse will vary enormously in the type and severity of the risks.

- It doesn't help plan the next steps. Too often, social work assessments recommend 'holding a child protection conference' as though that were an outcome in itself. While the conference may be necessary and may be a useful opportunity to coordinate plans, having a meeting doesn't inherently make someone any safer.

Instead, think 'what's happening in this person's life?' and 'what needs to happen to make this person safer?' The procedure should fit what needs to happen, not the other way around.

The link between protectiveness and risk

The Signs of Safety model popularised the use of strengths, protective factors, complicating factors and risks in statutory social work reports.

However, you lose the benefits of the model if you start creating 'lists' rather than exploring how the different factors link together.

There is a difference between a 'good thing' and a protective factor. There is a difference between a 'bad thing' and a risk factor.

Many assessments that partially use Signs of Safety end up with generic 'good' and 'bad' lists. The 'good' list might include:

- Immunisations are up-to-date.

- School attendance is good.

- Parents love their children.

- Family live nearby.

While the 'bad' list might include:

- Mother has suffered depression.

- Parents smoke cannabis.

- Father had a traumatic childhood.

- Child is behind at school.

- Parents don't want to work with professionals.

Any real 'risk' factor involves risk of harm (or risk of continuing harm) to a person. This is where the 'implication' part of the analysis is so important: does the father's traumatic childhood harm his children now? Does his cannabis use harm his children? Does the unwillingness to work with professionals *in itself* harm the children?

Often, a 'bad' factor may be a complicating factor rather than a risk factor. For example, the complicating factor may be that the parents smoke five joints of herbal cannabis per day, but the *risk* factor may be that while under the influence of cannabis, the parents fail to care for their children and leave them hungry and dirty. It is the impact on the children that constitutes the risk. Another parent may smoke just as much cannabis with no ill effects for their children. The unwillingness to work with professionals may be a complicating factor if they consequently don't work with someone who would be likely to help them make positive changes; in other cases, a wariness of professionals may make no difference to the outcome.

The same applies for the 'good' factors. If the reason for concern is that the father beats the mother in front of the children, the fact that they have had all immunisations is of no protective value. Having family nearby may be a strength, but it is only protective if those family members are actually able to keep the children safe from violence.

The point is that many factors are only 'risks' or 'protective' depending on the context. The circumstances of the individual case will affect what creates risk and protection for the people involved.

Always assume you're wrong

Klein (1999) recommends applying 'mental simulation' to risk assessment. Imagine that your prediction is wrong, reassess your analysis assuming it's wrong, and see where it could fall apart. This is much more effective than operating on the assumption that your conclusion is the right one.

Whatever you conclude, assume that it turns out to be wrong. Then examine your analysis to see 'where you went wrong'. Imagine being cross-examined after the situation has not turned out how you expected. This exercise is not designed to make you neurotic, but to encourage humility, nuance and an acceptance of the 'messiness' and unpredictability of some situations. This actually makes a case stronger rather than weaker: an analysis that recognises where it could be wrong but still considers one outcome likely has more integrity than one that only considers one possibility.

ANALYSIS AS A MEANS OF OPPRESSION OR EMPOWERMENT
Identity

Professionals can unwittingly and subtly oppress service users by redefining their identity in terms of the professional's model of assessment.

Calhoun (1995) describes the resulting 'categorical identity': 'the binary either/or logic that puts people or objects into categories, while obscuring the ambiguities'.

This can de-individualise the person – 'part of a pressure towards repressive sameness' – especially when coupled with the use of generic terms to describe the events in their lives (see **The dangers of 'categories'** in Chapter 4).

Calhoun (1995) describes this process of categorising as:

> **an act of taking unique, whole individuals apart, and then putting them together according to requirements of the system ... the creation of a 'virtual identity' has become essential to the functioning of contemporary society and, consequently, also an increasingly important part of contemporary forms of social control.**

Parton (2008) makes the worrying observation that 'knowledge which cannot be squeezed into the required format disappears or gets lost'. He echoes Calhoun:

> **social work increasingly acts to take subjects apart and then reassembles them according to the requirements of the database. Practitioners are required to produce dispersed and fragmented identities made up of a series of characteristics and pieces of information which are easy to input/output and compare. In the process, the embodied subject is in danger of disappearing and we are left with a variety of surface information which provides little basis for in-depth explanation or understanding.**

These two authors summarise the pitfalls of using a prescribed assessment format, particularly as part of a computer system. While a working knowledge of these formats can help you write your assessments more efficiently (see Chapter 4), the format should never *become* your assessment. Work out the analysis you need to write, then work out a way to best get this across within the format – don't allow the format to limit how you think about the service user.

This isn't necessarily a criticism of any particular template – the advice applies whether the format is well-designed or not (full disclosure: I advise a software company, helping them design a more user-friendly and service-user-focused data system for social workers), but a generic format can never predict every complexity about every service user you work with.

Bias and prejudice

Beware of your unconscious bias (see Chapter 4 regarding Project Implicit) and how it affects your analysis.

Particularly consider the role of social class in your assumptions. Social workers come from many different backgrounds, and social class has many definitions, but every social worker does professional-type work, and has a degree and a professional qualification. Many will also earn well above the national average wage (whether their earnings are good value for the work they do is an entirely different debate) and many own their own homes or will eventually do so. This combination of factors means that the social worker occupies a middle-class status in the minds of service users. This status can be abused:

> **despite many changes in the language and knowledge base since the end of the nineteenth century, social work remains an activity that is not only class specific, but also has continued to practice as if the primary causes of clients' problems are located in their behaviour, morality, and deficient family relationships**
>
> (Jones 2002)

Thompson (1997) uses the 'PCS' model to analyse discriminatory behaviour, showing how it occurs at the personal, cultural and societal level. A social worker can, without properly reflecting on their assumptions, bring all three levels into their work: their personal prejudices, the culture of their organisation, and the expectations of wider society.

Prejudices can make a difference in how you treat minor information. Consider these two cases:

Example 1

Mr Brown throttled his wife in front of his children and hit her several times causing a broken jaw. The local authority created a child protection plan.

Mr Brown refused to go to meetings to begin with. He told the social workers he shouldn't have hit his wife and won't do it again, but said he hates going to their office or meeting social workers.

Social workers have found the home untidy, cramped and sparsely furnished.

When the social workers tried to get him to go to a domestic violence programme with a six-month waiting list, he shouted and swore at the social workers about having to wait so long and then miss work. He also swore at school staff when they criticised him for picking up the children late after a meeting with the social worker.

Professionals are now worried about Mr Brown's aggressive behaviour and worry about his lack of engagement and the children's safety. Teachers describe the children as quiet and a bit grubby in school, although they say that at least their parents don't fight anymore. The local authority is taking legal advice about the prospect of going to court to compel Mr Brown to attend a violence programme.

Example 2

Mr Theobald throttled his wife in front of his children and hit her several times causing a broken jaw. The local authority created a child protection plan.

Mr Theobald sobbed in the meetings and told the social workers how terribly he regretted what had happened. His lawyer attended every meeting and was in regular contact with the local authority reminding them of their obligations.

Social workers' reports praise the beautiful condition of the family home, where both children have a range of musical instruments.

Mr and Mrs Theobald hired a psychiatrist to work with both of them around their relationship and with Mr Theobald on his anger issues.

All the professionals involved have been pleased with the response of the parents. The children say they are happier but just wish their parents didn't fight as much.

These cases involve the exact same reason for a child protection plan. Since then, Mr Brown's children say their parents don't fight anymore, while Mr Theobald's children say they wish their parents would stop fighting. And yet, professionals are far more relaxed in the Theobald case than the Brown case. Unwin and Hogg (2012) warn of the risks posed by an articulate, potentially intimidating service user, and missing the key factors. In this case, the social workers may be placing too much emphasis on apparent compliance, the state of the home and the family's resources.

Professionals become more worried about poorer, less-educated adults who are antagonised by professional processes than they are about articulate, well-presented adults who know how to 'jump through hoops'.

Social workers can allow prejudices around ethnicity, religion, gender, sexuality and disability to affect their analysis in similar ways. The process of analysis and the process of reflection cannot be separated: accurate, fair analysis requires that you reflect on *why* you are concerned (or not concerned) about a particular situation, and what factors are influencing your conclusion.

PERSONAL JUDGEMENTS

Judges ruling on both children's and adult's cases have frequently reminded the social work profession of the limits to their role, particularly when social workers object to aspects of a person's lifestyle.

In the Family Courts: Hedley (2007) ruled:

It matters not whether the parent is wise or foolish, rich or poor, educated or illiterate, provided the child's moral and physical health are not in danger. Public authorities cannot improve on nature.

He famously continued:

society must be willing to tolerate very diverse standards of parenting, including the eccentric, the barely adequate and the inconsistent. It follows too that children will inevitably have both very different experiences of parenting and very unequal consequences flowing from it. It means that some children will experience disadvantage and harm, while others flourish in atmospheres of loving security and emotional stability. These are the consequences of our fallible humanity and it is not the provenance of the state to spare children all the consequences of defective parenting. In any event, it simply could not be done.

Munby (2014) echoed this position in his admonishment of local authorities seeking to act as 'guardians of morality'. To separate a child from a family requires not only that the parents have taken poor decisions but that the children are likely to suffer significant harm in the future as a result.

In the court of protection: Jackson (2014) reminds adults' social workers: 'do not let the tail of welfare wag the dog of capacity'. People often make terrible, even life-threatening decisions, but they must be allowed to make them. To deprive someone of their liberty, the applicant cannot simply demonstrate why their decision is a bad one – they must show the service user lacks the capacity to make it.

Professionals have reported to me their 'concerns' about a parent including: being a gipsy, being home-schooled, having an open relationship, belonging to a 'fringe' religion, belonging to a 'fringe' political party, smoking cannabis, using alternative medicine, etc.

In different places or at different times, people might also have raised 'concerns' about someone being a single parent, being transsexual, being gay, being in a transracial relationship, being atheist, having a minority religion, having home births, breast-feeding, not breast-feeding, drinking alcohol, *not* hitting their children or having a relationship outside of marriage.

When you work with a service user, you will come to know intimate details of their lives. If professionals subjected each other to that level of scrutiny, they would doubtless find numerous aspects of each other's lives that they found appalling or unwise. But it wouldn't be their business to intervene.

Often, social workers become rightly involved in someone's private life because of something serious, but then become fixated on relatively minor problems. Sometimes social workers remain in a family's life even after the major issue has been resolved, because the minor issues remain, even though they would never have justified statutory involvement in themselves.

Always take a step back and ask 'what are the implications?' You will never create a 'risk-free' or perfect environment in a family, and you certainly shouldn't try to create such an environment in your own image.

AFTER THE ASSESSMENT: MAKING PLANS

Purpose and tone

Remember the outcome is what matters, not you completing a report.

Your plans should be based on your analysis. If you've identified a problem in your analysis, and the effect and cause of the problem, then the plan should be about addressing that cause and reducing its effects. Reder and Duncan (1999) and Turney et al. (2011) found a link between the outcomes for children and the closeness between the assessment and the plan.

Too often social work becomes removed from the needs of the community: 'the emphasis of anti-oppressive practice has often tended to be on changing the attitudes, behaviour and language of individual workers, as opposed to changing the conditions in which clients live' (Ferguson and Woodward 2009)

Make sure your plan is focused on improving someone's life, not justifying a professional role.

'Engagement' and blaming the service user

Canadian researchers Liebenberg et al. (2013) analysing social workers' case notes found a worrying trend towards 'responsibilisation': a tendency by social workers to blame a service user's problems on 'non-compliance', 'resistance' or 'lack of cooperation' rather than exploring environmental or institutional factors, and rather than allowing any challenge to the professionals' plans. They linked this to a neoliberal political culture that places the blame for dysfunction on the individual rather than organisations or social issues.

Continuing the theme of the previous section, the risk here is to use 'non-engagement' itself as a reason to raise the level of concern (and the level of intervention) in someone's life. The dangers are:

- That this can discriminate against those who don't understand professional processes. Better-educated and more articulate parents can be more adept at 'ticking the boxes' and demonstrating compliance, while the level of risk remains the same.

- The definition of 'engagement' can be loose. If the aim of a plan is to improve the living conditions at home, and the service user fails to attend some of the courses they are referred to but nevertheless transforms their home, this is more of an 'engagement' than someone who attends every appointment but doesn't change their behaviour.

- The plan can be undermined by hypocrisy. The same social workers writing scathingly about a service user's lateness at appointments might turn up an hour late for a home visit or cancel meetings at the last minute. The result is disillusionment for the service users and a lack of confidence in the professionals involved.

Plans can become an exercise in 'service users doing what they're told' rather than a means of improving someone's life, while a more systemic approach is needed.

An oppressive, one-sided analysis can frame a systemic or interactional problem solely in terms of the service user's 'fault': 'they haven't engaged with a service' (when the service runs a four-month waiting list or has closed); 'they are hostile to professionals' (when professionals have insulted them or let them down); or 'they have been very angry at social workers' (because the social worker told them to come to the office immediately and then kept them waiting for two hours). Recognising wider problems doesn't weaken your arguments, it shows fairness and improves the chances that your recommendations will be taken seriously.

Focus on what's important

Remember the difference between 'outcomes' and 'outputs'. A vulnerable person being made safer or happier is an outcome. A professional writing a report or attending a meeting is an output. Your plans should aim for outcomes, not outputs.

The following are not aims in themselves:

- holding a meeting

- writing an assessment

- doing visits

- arranging appointments

- sharing information.

Clearly, all of these things may be important in achieving an outcome, but they are the means and not the ends. When reviewing your plans, don't ask 'have all these visits happened?' (an easy question to answer) but 'is this person safe and well?', 'is the risk of X lower?', 'have we solved these problems?'

'SMART' (specific, measurable, attainable, relevant and time-bound) plans come from management consultancy through the technique of 'management by objectives' (Drucker 1954, honed by Doran 1981), and have gained popularity in local authorities. There are positives to draw from this approach: following the SMART criteria means saying *who* will do something (rather than just 'this task is to be done…'), when and why. However, the technique also risks being overly task-driven and losing track of what the overall plan is trying to achieve.

Beware of 'padding': you may feel more productive with 30 'things to do' on a safeguarding plan, but the dangers are:

- A lack of hierarchy: some tasks may be much more important to others and this may not come across.

- Setting the service users up to fail if the plan is too demanding and incoherent.

- A false sense of security: three months later, the professionals may be delighted that 29 out of 30 aims have been achieved, but the 30th might be 'Mr Jones not to hit his father', which was the original point of the plan.

- Irrelevance. For every element of a plan, ask: 'will the risks be reduced if this is achieved?' and 'if this is not achieved, will there be a risk of harm?' If the answer is 'no', seriously consider whether it should be in the plan.

A plan with one aim and one element is perfectly legitimate if that is all that is needed (although this is very rare). A plan with 100 elements for ten aims, on the other hand, may be no more effective and may actually be self-defeating.

CHAPTER SUMMARY

Analysis is about more than just the facts, but you first need to *have* the facts. Having gathered information, you need to analyse the likely truth of the information before analysing the overall issues.

When trying to unpick the truth:

- Acknowledge uncertainty but still give a view on what seems likely.

- Carry out 'parallel' analysis if necessary, showing the risks whether a disputed fact is true or not.

- Avoid words with truth-value overtones; for example, using 'was open about' or 'tried to claim' instead of just 'said'. Don't assume you can tell whether someone is telling the truth just by listening to them.

- Compare accounts against each other to spot inconsistencies.

- Take history into account, rather than basing everything on a recent conversation.

- Remember people can tell the truth in bad faith, or give incorrect information in good faith.

- Use a table to compare accounts if the case is complicated.

Be succinct:

- Your primary document (the statement or the assessment) should contain your train of thought, and cross-refer to long, detailed accounts on a lower 'level' of the Information Pyramid.

- Use your judgement to exclude information irrelevant to the argument you are making (this doesn't mean exclude information that *contradicts* your argument: you should include this, and acknowledge it).

In your analysis:

- Address causation and implication, as well as just information.

- Use practice models, where you understand them and where they are useful to understanding the case.

- Listen to your 'gut feeling' and see whether the evidence supports it. Your intuition will be guided by your practice wisdom.

- Quote research suitably.

- Don't be tempted to create a 'compromise reality' between what two people say, when doing so wouldn't make sense. If you think someone is lying or telling the truth, provide evidence.

- Don't be satisfied with showing how the case 'reaches a threshold' or 'fits criteria'. Work out what's happening in this specific case, and what needs to change, and how your systems and structures would help this happen. Don't categorise according to your systems and make the service user work around them.

- It's only a risk factor if it creates a risk of harm to someone, not if it's 'bad'.

- It's only a protective factor if it protects from a danger, not if it's 'good'.

- When you've reached a view, 'flip it round' and imagine it's completely wrong. If the evidence fits the opposite view, your conclusion is probably weak. If alternative views contradict the evidence, your conclusion is stronger.

Remember the oppressive power of analysis: how a rigid structure can redefine a real person in terms of an agency's process. Don't lose sight of the person at the heart of your assessment, and make the document fit around them rather than the other way around. Always reflect on your own bias and ask whether your judgements are really about harm and need or whether they reflect your own assumptions and prejudices.

Your plans should:

- Reflect your assessment.

- Focus on achieving required change, not on 'compliance'.

- Stay relevant to the needs and risk that you're trying to address.

EXAMPLE OF A TABLE TO WEIGH UP RELIABILITY

The following could be a section from an assessment. I would always create a table from scratch rather than create a standard 'template' for this exercise, since the format will be different depending on what you're analysing.

Disputed fact	What Mrs Smith says	What Mr Smith says	What Mr Bloggs says	What other information says
Whether Mr and Mrs Smith keep Mr Bloggs locked in the house alone for long periods.	'We never did that: we went out one time to get milk and didn't want him getting confused and wandering off, that was when the social worker came round [on 3 June]. We'd only been out for ten minutes.'	'There's always someone at home with Mr Bloggs, we've only ever left him with someone else there.'	On 3 June: 'I was scared, I didn't know where anyone was. I had enough food for a day but after two days I got hungry and the doors were all locked so I couldn't get food. That's when I banged on the windows till someone noticed me.' On 19 June: 'They've never left me alone, I don't remember being alone for more than five minutes when they went to get milk.'	A neighbour said on 3 June that Mr Bloggs was distressed and banging on the windows, saying he was hungry. The same neighbour told Social Services that she often saw Mr Bloggs looking out of the window with the house dark and no signs of anyone else home. The social worker on 3 June found a very dirty home and letters on the doormat.
Mr Smith gets drunk and hits Mr Bloggs	'My husband would never do anything like that. He's not a violent person, he's never hurt anyone.'	'That's a malicious and hurtful allegation. We love Mr Bloggs and I've never hurt him.'	On 3 June: 'I can't remember how [the black eye] happened, I think I must have fallen.' On 19 June: 'It wasn't Mr Smith who hit me, it was someone else. I can't remember who.'	Staff at the daycare centre say Mr Bloggs has arrived with a black eye three times, and never said how he did it. Mr Smith has three cautions for hitting Mrs Smith, twice when he was drunk. He was also in prison in 2009 for grievous bodily harm against a work colleague. A neighbour claimed on 24 June that Mr Smith is an alcoholic who always shouts at his wife and Mr Bloggs.

From the table above, I can infer that:

1. Although Mr and Mrs Smith and Mr Bloggs have all, at some point, said Mr Bloggs is not left alone, Mr Bloggs' words in the second interview are curiously similar to those used by Ms Smith. He has previously said, consistent with information from a neighbour, that he was left alone for a long time. The social worker finding letters on the doormat circumstantially contradicts Mr and Mrs Smith's claim that they had only been out for ten minutes. If Mr and Mrs Smith are telling the truth, then there is no explanation for the consistency between Mr Bloggs' initial account and the neighbour's. If they are not telling the truth, then this would suggest they may have influenced Mr Bloggs to give an account consistent with their own.
2. Mr Bloggs' claim that someone else hit him is confusing given that he spends all of his time either with Mr and Ms Smith or at the daycare centre (where no one has claimed he has been hit). Mr and Ms Smith's claim that Mr Smith has never been violent are contradicted by the fact of his previous cautions and convictions for hurting other adults. His criminal record and the neighbour's account are consistent with the suspicion that Mr Smith may have caused him injury, possibly when drinking alcohol.

TAKING IT FURTHER

Crittenden, P, Farnfield, S, Landini, A and Grey, B (2013) Assessing attachment for Family Court decision-making, *Journal of Forensic Practice*, 15(4), 237–248

Reder, P, Duncan, S and Lucey, C (2003) *Studies in the Assessment of Parenting*, Routledge

Teater, B (2014) *An Introduction to Applying Social Work Theories and Methods*, Oxford University Press

Turnell, A and Edwards, S (1999) *Signs of Safety: A Solution and Safety Oriented Approach to Child Protection Casework*, W.W. Norton & Company

REFERENCES

Ainsworth, M, Blehar, M, Waters, E and Wall, S (1978) *Patterns of Attachment*, Erlbaum

Berne, E (1964) *Games People Play: The Basic Handbook of Transactional Analysis*, Ballantine Books

Bowlby, J (1969) *Attachment and Loss*, Basic Books

Box, G E P (1976) Science and statistics, *Journal of the American Statistical Association*, 71, 791–799

Brandon, M, Belderson, P, Warren, C, Howe, D, Gardner, R, Dodsworth, J and Black, J (2008) *Analysing Child Deaths and Serious Injury Through Abuse and Neglect: What Can We Learn? A Biennial Analysis of Serious Case Reviews, 2003–2005*, Department for Children, Schools and Families

Brown, J and Duguid, P (2000) *The Social Life of Information*, Harvard Business School Press

Calhoun, C (1995) *Critical Social Theory: Culture, History and the Challenge of Difference*, Blackwell

Chapman, J (2004) *System Failure*, Demos

Crittenden, P and Landini, A (2011) *Assessing Adult Attachment: A Dynamic-Maturational Method of Discourse Analysis*, Norton

Dominelli, L (2002) *Anti-Oppressive Social Work Theory and Practice*, Palgrave Macmillan

Doran, G T (1981) There's a SMART way to write management's goals and objectives, *Management Review (AMA FORUM)*, 70(11), 35–36

Drucker, P (1954) *The Practice of Management*, HarperBusiness

Eriksson, A and Lacerda, F (2007) Charlantry in forensic speech science: a problem to be taken seriously, *International Journal of Speech Language and the Law*, 14(2), 169–193

Ferguson, I and Woodward, R (2009) *Radical Social Work in Practice: Making a Difference*, University of Chicago Press

Freire, P (1970) *Pedagogy of the Oppressed*, Bloomsbury

Hedley, J (2007) Re: L (Care: Threshold Criteria) [2007] 1 F.L.R. 2050

Jackson, P (2014) Heart of England NHS Foundation Trust v JB [2014] EWHC 342 (COP)

Jones, C (2002) Social work and society, in R Adams, L Dominelli and M Payne (eds.), *Social Work Themes, Issues and Critical Debates*, Palgrave Macmillan

Klein, G (1999) *Sources of Power: How People Make Decisions*, MIT Press

Liebenberg, L, Ungar, M and Ikeda, J (2013) Neo-liberalism and responsibilisation in the discourse of social service workers, *BJSW*, 45, 1006–1021

Lykken, D (1998) *A Tremor in the Blood: Uses and Abuses of the Lie Detector Test*, Plenum

Munby, J (2013) View from the President's Chambers (2): the process of reform: the revised public law outline and the local authority, *Courts and Tribunals Judiciary*, www.judiciary.gov.uk/wp-content/uploads/JCO/Documents/FJC/Publications/VIEW+FROM+THE+PRESIDENT.pdf

Munby J (2014) Judgement on Re. A [2015] EWFC 11

Munro, E (2004) *Effective Child Protection*, Sage

Nelson, D L, Reed, U S and Walling, J R (1976) Pictorial superiority effect, *Journal of Experimental Psychology: Human Learning & Memory*, 2, 523–528

Parton, N (2008) Changes in the form of knowledge in social work: from the 'social' to the 'informational', *British Journal of Social Work*, 38(2), 253–269

Parton, N and O'Byrne, P (2000) *Constructive Social Work: Towards a New Practice*, Macmillan

Platt, D and Turney, D (2013) Making threshold decisions in child protection, *British Journal of Social Work*, 44, 1472–1490

Prochaska, J O, Norcross, J C and DiClemente, C C (1994) *Changing for Good: The Revolutionary Program that Explains the Six Stages of Change and Teaches You How to Free Yourself from Bad Habits*, W. Morrow

Reder, P and Duncan, S (1999) *Lost Innocents: A Follow-Up Study of Fatal Child Abuse*, Routledge

Sagan, C (1980) *Cosmos*, Random House

Thompson, N (1997) *Anti-Discriminatory Practice*, Palgrave Macmillan

Turnell, A and Edwards, S (1999) *Signs of Safety: A Solution and Safety Oriented Approach to Child Protection Casework*, W.W. Norton & Company

Turney, D, Platt, D, Selwyn, J and Farmer, E (2011) *Social Work Assessment of Children in Need: What Do We Know? Messages From Research*, Department for Education

Tversky, A and Kahneman, D (1973) Availability: a heuristic for judging frequency and probability, *Cognitive Psychology*, 5(1), 207–233

Unwin, P and Hogg, R (2012) *Effective Social Work with Children and Families: A Skills Handbook*, Sage

6 Summary

THE CONTEXT OF YOUR ASSESSMENT

The report you write is not really what matters.

What matters is your *awareness*: of the political context of your role; of the societal and environmental context of the person you assess; and of how the person's life fits into this context.

What matters is your *understanding* of the person, of what to do next and how to help them. Your understanding of the person includes the 'why, what and so what' of their lives: what's happening, why it's happening and what the implications are.

A written report is not the centrepiece of your job. It is only a written snapshot, at a moment in time, of an understanding that keeps developing, within an awareness of the much wider context that shapes people's lives.

This book includes some practical tips for writing your report comprehensively, concisely and analytically. Without the ability to write a useful report, it's harder to focus on the key issues, and harder to sustain a useful plan. But a social worker knowing how to write a good report is like a politician knowing how to plan an election campaign, or an army officer knowing how to use a rifle, or a judge knowing how to memorise case law: indispensable skills, but only a means to an end, and inadequate without an understanding of the context they're working in. You are not a machine, and while you need to analyse and organise, you shouldn't do so mechanically.

The assessments you write are not politically neutral and neither are you. The kind of organisation you work for, the laws you work under, the processes you work through, the report template you use, the education and training you've had, and the way you practice, are all the result of political and moral decisions, and all of them perpetuate the values behind those decisions. Whether it's the neoliberal philosophy behind the privatisation of core social care services, or the management consultancy logic behind SMART plans, or the compartmentalising approach behind many assessment templates, these assumptions (whether good or bad) are built in to the environment you work in. That doesn't mean you have to accept them, but you need to be aware of them and recognise that your work has political significance.

STARTING YOUR ASSESSMENT

To develop an understanding of a person, and produce a good assessment, you need to read a lot. Create your chronology, create your genogram, and use these to start building a picture of the person's life. Develop hypotheses about why things happen the way they do, and to identify gaps in your knowledge.

Never write a document without knowing why you're doing it. The chronology and genogram are not administrative tasks to 'get out of the way' – they are a part of your assessment. Your chronology should tell a story. Your genogram and/or ecomap should be a picture of a family network.

If written at the start, a good chronology:

- uses, and later informs, your professional judgement;

- differs from case notes in their focus on the service user, and their ability to tell a story, summarise and reflect on events;

- saves time and avoids some basic analytical mistakes;

- improves the quality of your early visits.

See Chapter 2 for more on writing the chronology, and Chapter 3 for genograms and ecomaps.

Know why you're doing the assessment: 'because you've been told to' is not good enough. An assessment should have a purpose, usually to inform a decision: do you need to work with this person? Do they need statutory action to protect them? Does their plan need to change? Will a particular home or service be suitable for them?

GETTING THE WORK DONE

Everyone works differently. If you have a system that allows you to produce good, timely work, great. If you're struggling to manage your workload and to develop a timely understanding of the people you need to help, then Chapter 3 may be useful.

Key concepts

Knowing the service user, knowing what the problems are, and knowing what you want to do to help, will help your 'time management' better than any practical tips. This is because paperwork is easier when you know the people, while the reverse is not true: spending lots of time doing administration does not help you know the person any better. More time learning about a service user (through face-to-face meetings that you've prepared for, speaking to those who know them, reading relevant files) will make your written assessments quicker and of better quality.

I can't emphasise this enough, because so many social workers believe the myth of a 'trade-off' between time with service users and meeting deadlines. Spending time preparing for contact, having contact with someone and writing about it straightaway all seem very demanding. But they're all time investments (not to mention good practice): they consume more time initially, but they pay off over the course of your work. Fewer wasted visits, fewer unnecessary or repetitive meetings, fewer tasks needing to be redone, and less overall time coming to informed decisions, all save you time in the long-run.

The second damaging myth (linked to the first) is that spending more time means doing your job well and vice versa. There will always be long, unproductive working weeks for as long as people believe that there is *inherent* value in long hours (this is very different from working long hours to achieve something valuable, which so many social workers do every day). A four-hour meeting is not better than a one-hour meeting when the same aims are achieved. An assessment that takes 12 weeks is not better than one that takes three when they both reach the same conclusions with the same evidence and understanding. Staying until midnight helps a service user no more than leaving work at 5pm, if you haven't accomplished anything further. The result of this myth is that efficiency is confused with rushing, and promptness is viewed with suspicion.

Never rush. Just work out what you need to do, why you need to do it, and then do it. Rushing happens when you reach an external deadline and people are demanding a finished report.

So the following tips are not the key to getting work done. But they can help:

Practical suggestions

Keep yourself healthy

All other things being equal, you'll work better if you sleep, eat, and exercise better. This includes the discipline to *stop working*: after a certain number of hours per day (everyone's limit will be different) you'll produce minimal work of any use, and just keep reducing your health. Have the courage to stop work and come in the next morning refreshed.

Organise your everyday practice

Have a system for managing your emails, filing your documents and making the most of your smartphone (without taking risks with data security). Keep a detailed calendar, for your sake and your employer's. Finally, keep a tidy (which does not mean empty) workspace, not out of an obsession with uniformity, but because it increases your focus and ability to get the work done.

Have a system to organise your work

I find spreadsheets helpful, other people keep track of their cases on a paper notebook, some use a cloud-based system. However you do it, you need some kind of system to keep track of what you need to do and when. Knowing that you're behind with some things is far better than having no idea.

Get requests in early

When your work is dependent on another professional processing a referral or finding some information, make that request as early as possible. That reduces the risk of you completing all 'your' work, then waiting for them to reply. Make requests by email and chase them up.

Plan your visits and even your phone calls

Any conversation can take an unexpected turn, and it should never feel like going through a 'checklist', but you'll have more useful contact with people if you've prepared what you need to discuss. This doesn't mean being inflexible – quite the opposite. By making sure you talk about the important issues, you allow the possibility of more interesting, valuable conversations that lead on from those starting points.

Plan the nuts and bolts of your visits

Know your journey times, where the places are on a map and who's going to be where and when. Cutting out wasted visits and unnecessary travel time gains time and costs nothing. Where possible, see where you can do more than one visit to multiple people in the same area. Consider the aims of the visit, whether it should be announced or unannounced, and who you want to see at the same time or separately (family and professionals) and plan accordingly.

If you want to talk to someone, talk to them

Visits happen more reliably when you've talked to someone about it, arranged a time suitable for them and sent them a text reminder, compared to sending out an appointment letter and turning up with no further contact. Act like you want the visit to happen, and don't do the 'social worker knock'. Always be on time.

Write things thoroughly, but only write them once

Copy well-written summaries from case notes but otherwise cross-reference rather than copying. Hard as it sounds, writing case notes in detail, 'report-ready' immediately after every visit (or *during* each phone call) is a massive time-saver.

Deadlines are useful, but arbitrary ones are not

Set your own deadlines based on what you need to do, when you can do it, and how quickly the service user needs it done, and set them well within the 'official' deadlines. Think 'how long has this been going on?' rather than 'how long until the statutory deadline?'

Manage your office boundaries

Good relationships with colleagues are essential, and so is drawing on their wisdom and support. But everyone needs to 'tune out' sometimes. Work out what location, time of day and other aspects of your environment work best for you. Help your colleagues, but don't be afraid to (politely) distance yourself from a conversation that isn't helping anyone.

Don't let *fear* stop you working

You can only do good work by doing *something*, and whenever you do something, you can be criticised or attacked. This is how you learn and develop. By doing nothing, you create nothing 'wrong' but you remove any possibility of being 'right'. Understanding this can remove a major barrier to getting a report written.

WRITING AN ANALYTICAL REPORT

See Chapter 4 on writing style and Chapter 5 on analytical tips.

Writing concepts

- Always write with a reader in mind.

- Practice by writing for fun: you'll get more used to starting and finishing something, and writing simply.

- Use 'I' wherever relevant. You represent an organisation, but should always be accountable for your own observations and your own judgement.

- Become familiar with the prescribed templates, but only use them as a starting point. Different assessments will require different structures, and creating your own 'sub-headings' can help the flow of your argument.

Writing habits

- Avoid the passive voice. 'He did this' is better than 'it was done by him' or, worse, 'it was done'.

- Avoid generic terms for specific events. 'He hit her in the face with the edge of a plate, cutting her lip' is better than 'there was a domestic incident'.

- Avoid jargon. The words you use should act as 'real telepathy', transmitting the images and ideas in your head into someone else's head. Avoid words that tell you nothing. Don't worry about 'sounding professional' – you sound professional (and *are* professional) when you show that you understand a person, and understand how to communicate.

- Use people's *own words* to make a point, wherever possible. This is more authentic and carries a lot more power.

- Remember the oppressive power inherent in language. Don't ever treat your words as 'neutral', especially not when they have a bearing on someone's life. Your assessment will always be affected by your own assumptions and views – it will never be purely 'objective'. However, by keeping your language specific and analytical rather than vague and subjective, you can help reduce these effects.

To write analytically

- First know the facts, as far as possible. Keep a healthy, respectful scepticism about what you hear, and explore which information is consistent or inconsistent with other evidence, and what this means. Where the whole assessment hinges on a single uncertain fact, provide an analysis of the situation if the fact is true or if it is false.

- Don't use language with additional meaning if that's not the meaning you intended. 'He was open about...' suggests you believe him. 'He said' leaves open the truth of his words.

- Look beyond what you've seen and heard, and analyse the significance of what has happened when you weren't there, and in the past.

- Only include what's relevant. Where it is relevant, and there are multiple documents available to the reader, summarise a theme in one report rather than listing every event to support that theme. 'He has hit her 15 times in the last three years' is far more useful than listing every incident, provided you can provide references to the original information if required.

- Consider causation, information and implication: the 'why?', 'what?' and 'so what?' of a case. Having the information is important, but you only start analysing when you explore why things have happened, and what the implications have been (and what the implications will be in future).

- Use theoretical models where they are suitable and when you understand the model you're using. Cite research to support a wider point.

- Don't ignore your intuition (your 'gut feeling'), but see where it leads and whether the evidence supports it.

- Create an unbroken 'train of thought' from the primary evidence (who said what/ who did what) through your analysis (why these things happened, what they mean for everyone involved, what's likely to happen in future) to your conclusions and recommendations (therefore this needs to happen, here's how we can do it, etc.).

- Avoid the temptation to 'fudge' your analysis with a 'compromise reality' and don't replace a detailed, specific analysis of a particular person with a generic conclusion about 'meeting a criteria' or placing them in a broad category.

- Link protectiveness to risk, and analyse both sets of factors in terms of what happens. Many factors may or may not be risks, or protective, depending on the details and depending on the circumstances.

- Imagine how you'd justify your analysis if you turned out to be wrong. Assume that the correct conclusion was the opposite of what you've written, then see if the evidence fits this conclusion too. If it does, this calls your conclusion into question. If the evidence wouldn't fit any likely scenario except yours, this strengthens your argument.

- Resist the temptation to shape someone's identity into the structure of the assessment format or your organisation's processes.

- Be aware of your own biases and any other agenda within your organisation or profession, and recognise them in your thought process. Reflect on whether your conclusion reflects your own personal view of what is 'normal' or 'appropriate' or whether the evidence genuinely suggests a danger of harm.

- Keep your plans focused on the needs and risks involved, and avoid distractions.

Most of all, never stop challenging. Challenge yourself: can you do this better? What assumptions are you making about people? Challenge service users: be honest and straightforward when talking about a problem or what needs to change. Challenge your organisation: it's easy to criticise what previous workers did, but what about the things you and your colleagues are doing right now? Finally, challenge the assumptions made by the profession and society at large.

If you challenge yourself enough, you'll become more comfortable when other people challenge you – indeed, you may already have the answer. No one should ever be afraid of constructive criticism: it can either be correct (in which case it's a good thing you've heard it) or incorrect (in which case you get to practice showing why).

Good luck, and give it your best shot.

C. Dyke, February 2016

Writing for child care proceedings

This is the only section of the book aimed exclusively at statutory children's social workers, specifically those working in the Family Courts. It focuses mainly on the local authority social work evidence template for care proceedings, but first discusses other documents in brief.

The most significant analytical documents you submit to court (whether written by you or someone else) will probably be:

- the 'Statement' or local authority social work evidence template, discussed below: one document covering all the children involved in these proceedings;

- chronology;

- care plan(s): one for each child;

- child and family assessment (the same one you'd write for a non-court case): this should stand as the main assessment of the child's needs and of the parents' ability to care;

- parenting assessment(s): ideally, this should be unnecessary if the child and family assessment explores and analyses parenting in detail;

- special guardianship or similar assessments of alternative carers, for instance family members who are putting themselves forward to care for a child if the parents cannot.

I could not do justice to all these reports in one appendix, but see **Taking it further** for excellent guides to parenting assessment (Reder et al. 2003; Ostler 2008; Scaife 2012).

DETAILED REPORTS FOR CHILD CARE PROCEEDINGS: SPECIAL GUARDIANSHIP AND PARENTING ASSESSMENTS

Further issues may come up for parenting and special guardianship assessments, including:

The format/template for a parenting assessment

Opinions vary, and your organisation may have its own template for parenting assessments. However, in my view there shouldn't be one.

A parenting assessment, commissioned *in addition to* the child and family assessment, is designed either to:

1.   provide an independent view, outside of the local authority, or
2.   supplement the child and family assessment with exploration or analysis that the original assessment didn't cover. A comprehensive, up-to-date child and family assessment *should* make a parenting assessment unnecessary.

If 1, then an independent social worker will be guided by the letter of instruction that spells out what questions to answer. In this case, the author will use their judgement to determine a format (unless they work for a large agency, which require their own).

If 2, then there is already a structured assessment that addresses parenting. So your structure for the parenting assessment will depend on what the child and family assessment left out. If, for example, the parenting assessment is required because the original assessment analysed the parents' basic care in detail but didn't explore the violence between them, then the parenting assessment can cross-reference the original assessment regarding basic care, but focus in detail on violence.

Be wary of any request to 'do a parenting assessment' when you have just done a child and family assessment and where you are given no other questions. As ever, always know *why* you're doing an assessment and what it's supposed to cover.

If you're writing a parenting assessment for court, you may find it useful to ask the guardian for their views on what areas should be included (although you should never try to coordinate or influence their opinions). If all parties have contributed to your list of questions, then you cannot reasonably be asked to rewrite it if you have competently answered those questions.

The difference between an assessment of a foster carer and a kinship carer

At the time of writing, new regulations have just been announced (Special Guardianship (Amendment) Regulations 2016), emphasising the need to focus on an applicant's ability to care for a child to the age of 18, and their past and current relationship with the child.

Research on special guardianship found (Selwyn et al. 2014; Wade et al. 2014) that while placements with a family member under a special guardianship order rarely break down, they are more likely to break down than adoptive placements. Particular risk factors include:

•   Frequent changes of placement prior to a special guardianship order being made.

•   The applicant not being biologically related to the child.

•   'Children who came into care due to family reasons such as acute stress, family dysfunction, socially unacceptable behaviour, low income, absent parenting were nearly twice as likely to face a disruption compared with children who came into care due to abuse or neglect' (Selwyn et al. 2014).

- The child not having previously been cared for by the applicant.

- Lack of a strong existing relationship with the applicant.

- Applicants who have been 'pushed' into applying by the family.

More generally, social workers can confuse the analysis of would-be special guardians with the analysis of would-be foster carers or adopters. While in both cases the carer needs to be able to provide safe, warm, long-term care for a child, their circumstances are different since the special guardian has a link to the child's family.

This doesn't mean your assessment of a family member should be either more or less rigorous than an assessment of a stranger. It means it should be different. Some applicants would not be accepted as foster carers or adopters, but *would* be suitable as special guardians *for a particular child*. Similarly, some applicants would make good foster carers or adopters, but could not care for this particular child under these circumstances.

Example 1

Mr Muhammed has been in prison twice in his 20s for fighting with other adults while he was a drug addict. He is now 45 and teetotal for 15 years. He does casual jobs and was declared bankrupt ten years ago. He is very close to his nephew Akash (14), who can no longer live with his parents and has experienced the breakdown of five foster placements. Akash wants to live with Mr Muhammed and has stayed with him for several months before social services tried to return him to his parents.

Example 2

Ms Donald is a high-earning professional with a clean criminal record, who raised two of her own children to adulthood with no difficulties. She has been put forward as an alternative carer to her great-niece Claire (7). Claire has never lived with Ms Donald and only seen her on visits. Claire has suffered serious abuse and displays a wide range of violent and distressing behaviour, causing the breakdown of three foster placements. Ms Donald is scared of Claire's parents, who live near her, but she does not want to move and lose her community.

Depending on the details, it is plausible that Mr Muhammed may not be approved as a foster carer or adopter for children he has never met, while Ms Donald may make an excellent candidate. However, for these specific relationships, Mr Muhammed may well be the best carer for Akash, and Ms Donald may be unsuitable as a carer for Claire through no fault of her own.

You are not just assessing a *person*, you are assessing a *situation* and a *relationship*.

WRITING A STATEMENT UNDER THE NEW PUBLIC LAW OUTLINE

You can find the blank template at http://adcs.org.uk/care/article/SWET. This Appendix covers the practical side of getting your statement written for care proceedings. See **Taking it further** for more thorough guides to court work.

All the previous advice about analysis and report-writing applies, but now you're writing for the 'top' of the Information Pyramid. Your statement should make an argument, not list every fact.

Take care to *balance* your evidence: a judge is more impressed by analysis that recognises the complexity of the case and all the evidence against your position, as well as the evidence in favour. Admitting the points that work against you actually strengthens your case rather than weakening it.

The New Public Law Outline means:

* as much as possible done *before* issuing proceedings;

* 'a smaller amount of more analytical material';

* filing all 'annex' documents at the point of issuing (statement, chronology, care plan), and having all 'checklist' documents (other assessments, reports by other professionals, etc.) ready to share if requested;

* expert assessments already completed before issuing, if possible;

* the clock starts ticking from the day of issuing. By Day 12 you need to have a full hearing.

Think about the document as a *conversation with the judge*, with each section forming your side of the conversation:

> **Judge: So who are you and who are you talking about?**
>
> **You: I'm ..., your honour, and I'm here about John and his family [Section 1.1–1.3].**
>
> **Judge: And what are you doing here?**
>
> **You: Your honour, we'd like you to give us an interim care order to protect John from violence. We don't think there's any other way to keep him safe [Section 1.4].**
>
> **Judge: So what's the story?**

You: Your honour, here's what's been happening in John's life... [Section 2].

Judge: I see. So why do you think he'll be at risk?

You: Well your honour, if he stays at home he's likely to be hurt in among the fighting between his parents [Section 3].

Judge: But what effect does that have on him?

You: He's been injured already, your honour, and if he stays there he'll probably be hurt again. At the very least, he's likely to suffer emotional trauma as he has already [Section 4].

Judge: Oh dear. But can't the parents sort this out?

You: His parents don't seem able to do that, your honour – these fights have gone on for years despite our efforts to help them improve their relationship. If anything, it's getting worse. Here are the parenting assessments we wrote about them... [Section 5].

Judge: That's a shame. But surely there are other family members who can look after him?

You: We've assessed his grandmother and aunt, your honour, but neither of them could manage. Here are some reports we wrote about them... [Section 6].

Judge: So if I give you an Order, what will you do with it?

You: We've weighed up all the options, your honour, and we think a long-term foster placement is the best option for John. Here's our reasoning... [Section 7].

Judge: And what does everyone else think of this?

You: The parents are opposed, your honour, and they say we're wrong about... His aunt and his grandmother both think he's not safe there, but they'd rather he was with his wider family. John says he isn't sure what he wants [Section 8].

Judge: And have you treated the parents fairly?

You: Yes your honour... [Section 10].

Treating the statement as a 'conversation' helps keep you focused on the need to be clear, concise and analytical in your writing. Imagine you're actually speaking to the judge as you write: in the witness stand, you wouldn't read out the entire set of police reports to the judge, so you wouldn't write them in your statement. You would, however, refer to those reports and have them available – the option to 'go down the levels' of the pyramid if required.

SECTION-BY-SECTION GUIDE

Section 2: Court chronology

The court is mainly interested in the **last two years**' events. Significant information prior to that can be summarised, for example: '2003–2008: Mrs Jones' three older children were subject to child protection plans and care proceedings due to serious neglect and Mrs Jones' heroin habit. All three were placed in care in 2013 where they remain.'

See Chapter 2 for more on chronologies.

Section 3: Analysis of harm

This section is not about 'what has happened' (information) but what the effect has been on the child (implication).

Analyse the risk of harm to the child *given the individual needs of the children*. For example, Kyle (2) may be at high risk of significant harm from neglect due to his mother's drinking habits, while Julie (15) can take care of her own needs but gets angry and depressed when her friends taunt her.

> **Bad: 'There have been five domestic incidents between mother and father.'**

> **Good: 'John's father accidentally hit him while his mother held him, causing bruising, during at least one fight between his parents. Due to both of the parents drinking and being unable to control their temper, they have not been able to consider his safety, increasing the chances of him being hurt. The risk of further harm is even higher: the fights appear to be getting more serious with the inclusion of implements. John was a few feet away from his mother when his father hit her with a mug breaking her nose, and it is likely he will be hurt in future: research* shows that a quarter of children exposed to violence will try to intervene as they get older, increasing the danger further, and that half will suffer post-traumatic stress. John has suffered, and is at high risk of suffering, emotional and physical harm at home.'**

*Refuge (2005): Refuge assessment and intervention for pre-school children exposed to domestic violence www.refuge.org.uk/cms_content_refuge/attachments/Effects%20 of%20domestic%20violence%20on%20pre-school%20children.pdf.

Section 4: Child impact analysis

- Must address *each* child individually, in the same report.

- Should *not* duplicate information from other sections or reports – cross-refer to them where appropriate.

- Addresses (in Section 4.1) the 'day-to-day life' of each child: *you are the expert on the child* and this is your chance to show it.

- Addresses (in Section 4.2) the children's needs. This will overlap with a good assessment, so cross-referencing may be required. For example, 'I refer to my child assessment dated 24.11.2014 for a detailed analysis of Jack's needs. In summary, he is a shy and withdrawn six-year-old who finds it hard to make friends or talk about his feelings, to the point where his school are applying for a diagnosis of a social and communication disorder. These needs seem to have intensified during the six months since Mr Bloggs returned to the family home.'

- Addresses (in Section 4.3) the children's wishes. Use their *own words* as far as possible (there is also a Section, 4.4, for the child's own statement): for example, rather than saying 'Jamie was open about his concerns about his mother and verbalised that he wanted her to get better', say 'Jamie said: "I get saddest of all when mummy cries and drinks wine." [if he had one wish] "I'd like mummy not to drink and for mummy to feel better."'

- Considers (in Section 4.6) whether further assessments or delays would help the child. Sometimes they would, for example: 'A further three-month delay would leave Jimmy suffering continued uncertainty and anxiety over what is going to happen to him. However, as there is a reasonable likelihood of Mrs Smith remaining drug-free and providing good care (according to the recent psychiatric report dated 12.12.2016), a period of maintenance and continued drug counselling could result in a safe return home. The benefits to Jimmy of achieving this would, in my view, outweigh the unhappiness he would experience as a result of the delay.'

Section 5: Analysis of parents' capacity, and Section 6: Analysis of wider family and friends' capacity

For the parents, analyse:

- what the *gap* is between what the child needs (including safety from abuse) and what each parent can offer;

- What the *likelihood of closing that gap* is, in a reasonable time for the child.

For example, if a parent lacks basic care skills and doesn't understand her child's needs, does she have the cognitive functioning to absorb and implement these skills if offered the right parenting help (include whether she has been offered this before), or would the situation probably be no different in six or 12 months' time?

The court expects you to:

1. Try to reunite children with their parents.
2. If 1 is unfeasible, to place children with relatives or other people they know.

In both cases it is up to you to show whether this is the case, and if not, why not. A carer needs to be able to keep a child safe and offer 'good enough' parenting; they do not need to be perfect.

Section 7: The proposed s31A care plan: the 'realistic options' analysis (the 'Re. B-S' compliance check)

'Re. B-S' (Munby 2013) is an important precedent where the court confirmed that the local authority has to weigh up the pros and cons of each option and, if you are advocating permanent removal from the family, demonstrate why all the other options are unsuitable.

It is not enough to say 'mother is unable to keep Jane safe and is unlikely to make sufficient changes within Jane's timeframe, therefore we are seeking to have Jane adopted'. Instead, before concluding that adoption is the best outcome, you must show why (for example):

- mother cannot provide care;

- father is uncontactable *despite all these efforts* or is also unable to provide care;

- the family members put forward are not viable carers;

- long-term foster care would, on balance, not be as good an option.

Only 'reasonable' options need to be considered (for example, not adoption for a 17-year-old).

Section 8: Analysis of views and issues raised by other parties

This is a good opportunity to pre-empt potential challenges. For example:

Mrs Jones accepts that her parenting is not good enough at the moment, but says that with a parenting programme she might be able to care for Jenny within six months. However, I note that she has previously attended three different parenting programmes, and has been aware of your concerns for the past five years, without any sustained changes. The local authority does not support a delay to proceedings for this piece of work to take place, as I believe the chances of success are minimal and the delay in achieving permanence for Jenny would cause her increased instability and anxiety.

Section 9: Case management issues and proposals

Specific issues such as reasons for delay, special points to take into consideration, further reports needed.

Section 10: Statement of procedural fairness

This is your declaration that you have been fair to the parents and other key people involved: that they have been made aware of proceedings, given the chance to take legal advice, and have been aware of your concerns for a long time; for example, pre-proceedings work.

This is where the importance of pre-proceedings work comes in: courts criticise you in cases where they agree a threshold is reached but feel you have not given the parents enough of a chance to make changes. In some cases, this can even affect whether you get a care order: a court may decide that with a bit more work, the parents can close that 'gap' between their current and required levels of parenting.

THE CARE PLAN

This is what you are proposing to do if you are given a care order. In some cases, it may also spell out your plans for rehabilitation under a supervision order.

You need to write one per child (even though some areas may overlap – this is the one time when some of the text will be very similar, especially if they are placed together or returning home together).

Don't duplicate. Make reference to previous care plans if appropriate. If writing a new care plan for an existing court case, refer to the original plan and focus on areas where this care plan is different – the court have already read all the text in the first plan and don't need to read it again.

Match needs to plans: if we've identified that a child has specific needs, make sure the care plan shows how you will meet them.

Again, the work done *before* writing the document makes a difference: a court is impressed by how well you know the case and how much work you've done with the family. If you're proposing work with another service, *make the referral!* If you're proposing a specific assessment, make sure you've agreed it and written the letter of instruction.

Finally, upload everything to your data systems. It's very embarrassing for later social workers to have to ask the parents for a copy of your documents.

TAKING IT FURTHER/REFERENCES

Davis, L (2014) *The Social Worker's Guide to Childrens and Families Law*, 2nd edn, Jessica Kingsley

Douglas, A, Webb, A and Pickup, S (2013) *Good Practice Guide for Social Work Practiced in the Family Court*, ADCS/CAFCASS, www.cafcass.gov.uk/media/126324/good_practice_guidance_for_social_work_practised_in_the_family_courtsv5.pdf

Munby, J (2013) Re. B-S (Children) [2013] EWCA Civ 1146

Ostler, T (2008) *Assessment of Parenting Competency in Mothers with Mental Illness*, Brookes Publishing

Reder, P, Duncan, S and Lucey, C (2003) *Studies in the Assessment of Parenting*, Routledge

Scaife, J (2012) *Deciding Children's Futures: An Expert Guide to Assessments for Safeguarding and Promoting Children's Welfare in the Family Court*, Routledge

Selwyn, J, Wijedasa, D and Meakings, S (2014) *Beyond the Adoption Order*, University of Bristol School for Policy Studies, Department for Education

Special Guardianship (Amendment) Regulations (2016) Statutory Instrument 2016, no 111

Wade, J, Sinclair, I, Stuttard, L and Simmonds, J (2014) *Investigating Special Guardianship: Experiences, Challenges and Outcomes*, Department for Education

Index